What No One Tells the Mom

Here's to the
wild world of
motherhood!
Marg Stark

What No One Tells the

Mom

Surviving the Early Years of Parenthood with Your Sanity, Your Sex Life, and Your Sense of Humor Intact

Marg Stark

A Perigee Book

THE BERKLEY PUBLISHING GROUP
Published by the Penguin Group
Penguin Group (USA) Inc.
375 Hudson Street, New York, New York 10014, USA
Penguin Group (Canada), 10 Alcorn Avenue, Toronto, Ontario M4V 3B2, Canada
(a division of Pearson Penguin Canada Inc.)
Penguin Books Ltd., 80 Strand, London WC2R 0RL, England
Penguin Group Ireland, 25 St. Stephen's Green, Dublin 2, Ireland (a division of Penguin Books Ltd.)
Penguin Group (Australia), 250 Camberwell Road, Camberwell, Victoria 3124, Australia
(a division of Pearson Australia Group Pty. Ltd.)
Penguin Books India Pvt. Ltd., 11 Community Centre, Panchsheel Park, New Delhi–110 017, India
Penguin Group (NZ), cnr. Airborne and Rosedale Roads, Albany, Auckland 1310, New Zealand
(a division of Pearson New Zealand Ltd.)
Penguin Books (South Africa) (Pty.) Ltd., 24 Sturdee Avenue, Rosebank, Johannesburg 2196, South Africa
Penguin Books Ltd., Registered Offices: 80 Strand, London WC2R 0RL, England

PRINTING HISTORY
Perigree trade paperback edition / April 2005

PERIGEE is a registered trademark of Penguin Group (USA) Inc.
The "P" design is a trademark belonging to Penguin Group (USA) Inc.

Library of Congress Cataloging-in-Publication Information

Stark, Marg.
What no one tells the mom : surviving the early years of parenthood with your sanity, your sex life, and your sense of humor intact / by Marg Stark
p.   cm.
ISBN 0-399-53081-9
1. Motherhood.   2. Mother and child.   3. Love.   4. Marriage.   I. Title.

HQ759.S673 2005
306.874'3—dc22   2004057297

PRINTED IN THE UNITED STATES OF AMERICA

10   9   8   7   6   5   4   3   2   1

To my teachers,
Patrick and Liam

Contents

the secrets

1. Put out the welcome mat for your new friends, Obsession and Irrationality. Babies bring out the love and lunacy in all of us.

2. Blissed-out bonding is rare; annoyance is common. That's what love is like.

3. A new mom's spirits are not necessarily bright. Lighten up. Know that you're normal, and that "wonder babies" are a farce.

4. Motherhood today is mission impossible. Learn to love your real self the way your kids do. Then get in a huddle.

5. The work/life balance is elusive—for all moms. Choose the right mix for you and your family, and reevaluate frequently.

6. Moms lose a sense of self but amass life meaning in spades.

7. To grow great families, moms need to feel connected—to others and to the divine.

8. Men are slower to transform, but transform they must for marriage and family life to thrive.

9. Women do more because we are extraordinarily talented, patient and energetic. Demand the help of husbands, and let the rest go.

10. Romance is difficult to come by in these years but there are ways to lure pleasure from its hiding place.

11. Good people and good marriages can get waylaid by stress. Instead of turning on each other, be a team.

12. A downgraded marriage is fine for family life.

13. Admire and celebrate how far you've come.

14. Change your mind. Take baby steps.

I'm a Mess, We're a Mess...
Happily Ever After

❧ Before we embarked on the odyssey of parenthood, my husband, Duke, and I perceived ourselves as passionate and defiant. We stroked this ideal of us the way one would a loud-purring cat.

A first-time mom at thirty-three, I didn't worry about the personality thief that motherhood can often be. As a writer, I was blessed to have a career I could pursue at home while tickling the toes of my treasured baby. High energy and better at juggling multiple duties than many people I knew, I thought I might sneak smugly past the societal billboard that screamed "You *cannot* have it all."

With our zesty marriage, Duke and I were sure we could "settle down and have kids" without succumbing to the suburban clichés of cul-de-sac living and minivan ownership. No stodgy gender definitions or lopsided household work for us. We would rewrite marital and family history before we would permit inequity in our relationship.

Our Fantasy Family

Duke and I planned to inculcate our children to this rebel cause, a circle of fantastic love and possibility. Inside the picket fence and shuttered windows, our family of four or five would boogie to James Brown songs in the living room. Mother and son would be flinging long strands of pasta at the wall, long after al dente had been confirmed. And at a moment's notice, toddlers would get strapped into car seats, sleeping bags tossed into the Land Cruiser, simply because we'd never before experienced a campfire as a family. We had this formula for happiness we were so eager to share with children.

Personally, I believed I would never be forced to choose. I would never (as many women in magazine surveys did) credit my children with being my greatest source of satisfaction—over that of my husband or my writing career. No, some combination of these factors would leave me brimming. I imagined editors calling during a baby's naps, I imagined abundant vigor—and mental clarity—for everything, and dropping into bed at night with the peace of a life fully lived.

Welcome to the Real World

As you might imagine, this hippest of fairy tales did not materialize. To be perfectly honest, we tanked. Duke and I attacked the obstacle course with the zeal of Marines, seizing the ropes and planting our steel-toe boots for a quick ascent to bliss. But even now, seven years after the birth of our first son, we are tending to our rope-burned thighs. We are embarrassed at flailing so, and of underestimating the monstrous incline we had, and still have, before us.

Like the one hundred moms interviewed for this book, we eagerly desired a child and considered his birth the happiest day of our lives. Like many of us who became parents later than those of previous generations, Duke and I believed we would have trouble conceiving, and considered our Patrick "a miracle baby."

We brought our miracle bundle home to a tidy, two-income household with a solid marriage, made up of two resilient loving partners and a beloved Chesapeake Bay retriever—our first baby. Yet, within no time it was Dysfunction Central. Two weeks postpartum, stress and exhaustion were so pervasive I hurled a cordless phone at a wall, shattering it. In a month, Duke was alienated from our newborn—sure it was his arrival home from work not the famed infant "witching hour"—that turned little Patrick into a wailing, colic-ridden tyrant.

In nine months, my inability to bring in enough income, working part-time and paying for part-time child care, had Duke and I so on-edge we alternatively screamed at, or stopped talking to one another. Eighteen months later, I was in a therapist's office, reaching for tissue after tissue. And the dog? Her extinction was a distinct possibility.

You Are Not Alone

Marriage experts say that this is a textbook example of the ways in which most couples respond to the addition of, and care for, a new baby. Marital satisfaction plummets for two-thirds of American couples when they become parents.

A sobering statistic, I hit my marks the way scientists agree new mothers most often do. I crashed emotionally right along with my hormones in the days after I delivered this beautiful boy. Bony as he was, Patrick needed more milk than my breasts could produce, and needed Mommy to be calmer than he was in his colic-ridden state.

In the cozy corner of the dining room, where I had set up my office, productivity quickly proved impossible in the presence of my baby. Yes, wonder-welfare mother J. K. Rowling wrote feverishly in British coffeehouses, pram in tow. But I could not do both. I could not balance it—the combination of babies and ambitions—that I had, a year prior, chided a friend for being incapable of juggling. So I did the next logical thing: I had another baby, a second gorgeous son whom we named Liam.

Duke and I did preserve some of our dreams, some of those fairy-tale elements. We introduced James Brown gyrations to our offspring, launched linguini at the kitchen cabinets, and delighted in the way a dancing campfire reflected in our wee ones' eyes. But we did so bleary-eyed and exhausted, prone to caustic arguments and brooding. Each of us harked back to the leisure and independence we enjoyed prior to having children, and grew increasingly ashamed, since our grieving surely proved we didn't love Patrick and Liam the way "good parents" should.

Like many of the après-baby marriages on which we spied for this book, Duke and I sometimes wished away the years our elders told us were so precious. Right in front of us, a two-year-old's naked bottom toddled around the yard, ecstatic at the spray of water from a garden hose, at the largesse of life a molded plastic baby pool represented to him. In spite of being in the presence of a little Adonis, we kept checking our watches, so eager were we for the cessation of responsibility that came, briefly, at naptime.

Ironically, at the time our marriage might have been closest, we were, as individuals, totally out of sync. My wonder-mother friend

Kelly, the one who never seems stymied by parenthood, remembers a year after her son was born, a profound revelation occurred in the aisles of JCPenney. Kelly and her husband strayed from the main aisle at the same time, she to the baby section to coo over the clothes, he to the lingerie section to hold up items enticing to him. "We were on such different wavelengths. He wanted our marriage back—the steamy, spontaneous one. I just wanted to bask in the feeling of being a mother, of loving my son. That's when our weekly date nights started, and we've been having them for fifteen years now."

A full third of couples will glide through this adjustment period without a major need to reassess or realign. About a fifth of the first-time moms I interviewed also feel explicitly happy about the changes parenthood has brought. But there's an increasingly vocal group of parents—just tune in to *Oprah* and you'll hear them—who are overwhelmed by the demands of modern family life, conflicted about the yearnings of their hearts, and guilty about having mixed feelings when they love their children as they do.

Redeeming Truths

In the pages that follow, then, are observations and lessons drawn from the ranks of both the unequivocally delighted and the thoroughly conflicted. Contented couples have valuable lessons to share, as does a larger contingent of parents who consider themselves hilariously dysfunctional.

To acquire these nitty-gritty truths, we asked ourselves, our friends, and their friends—and a few important marriage researchers, therapists, child psychiatrists, and sex experts—wicked questions such as these:

- How do modern couples—more apt to be dual income and to be older than previous generations of parents—embrace the sacrifices of parenthood for which we are ill prepared?

- How can those of us accustomed to "cyberspeed" and "multitasking" slow ourselves down and find some inherent pleasure in the unfathomable rapture a toddler experiences in an hour-long focus on light switches?

- Why is it, exactly, that record numbers of women—including moms who adopt babies—experience postpartum depression? Why do some mothers with babies or young children appear to have it all together? And why do some moms seem utterly thrashed by the experience?

- Where did my previously healthy sex drive go? Are our libidos having a rocking orgy without us on some other planet?

- What did Gloria Steinem mean when she said that motherhood, not marriage, is the ultimate obstacle for feminists today?

- If I'm completely detached from my husband now, how will this marriage recoup itself when the children are older?

- How will my children's psyches be affected if I am, in truth, disappointed in the quality of life parenthood affords me?

A Book for Women, Wives, and Mothers

I've written this book for mothers, and the vast majority of the sources on whom I have relied are women. Of course husbands and dads are jolted when children are added to the mix, and they've told me that, too. But research shows that women experience the more dramatic metamorphosis.

You'll notice that my girlfriends and I are often tough on fathers in this book, and that we make derogatory generalizations about the way this species responds in this fateful transition to parenthood. Let me make my blanket apology to all the great dads I offend here, as most of you are contributing much more than your fathers did, and a percentage of you are phenomenal dads, better than many moms at meeting your children's voracious needs. But this book is about, and for, the ladies—so step aside, gentlemen.

The mothers I talked to range from twenty-two to forty-six, most but not all are college-educated and middle-class. They're from diverse religious and ethnic backgrounds. Most are married but some are single, divorced, living together, or in lesbian partnerships. Many work, either full-time or part-time, and others "stay at home," a term I'm forced to use until someone—*please, someone!*—comes up with a better name for these unpaid slave laborers who are always on the go. Nonetheless, all the moms in this book are identified by pseudonyms so as to ensure their complete candidness.

These moms have between one and six children, and have welcomed a new youngster into their lives within the last seven years so their memories are fresh and lively. My cohorts became mothers in every possible way: plain old sex or through in vitro fertilization, adoption and surrogacy, marrying someone with children or being a foster parent. New stepmoms will relate to some of these harrowing tales but their experiences proved too distinct from those of other moms for me to cover thoroughly. There are nuggets in the book for single moms, but considerable attention is given to the postpartum marriage.

Women Who Are Forever Changed

As Katherine Hadley said, "The decision to have a child is to accept that your heart will forever walk around outside your body." The utter vulnerability and inability to be the person you were before you became a mom is very disquieting to most of us, determined as we are to live independently, under control, and well-put-together.

So come with me, you tired and poorly groomed mamas. Let's celebrate this absurd, precious time. Don't worry that naming the disadvantages of this life means you love your children or your husband too little. Just commit to a frankness modern mothers are often frowned upon for admitting. Let the authentic, un-thwarted person you are, separate of children or husband, come out and play.

Then, in the fellowship of women who are as stressed-out as you are, we'll figure out together how to retain a sense of humor, and some bits of inner self. How to be lighter-hearted and surer-footed melding marriage and family life, without feeling that our pleasure in life is indefinitely on hold. There is deep pleasure to be mined in this time, and important planning to be made for your future—as a couple, as a family, and ultimately, as your true and emphatic self.

chapter one

Damn It, I'm Supposed to Be Serene!

Adjusting to the Idea of Pregnancy and Motherhood

> SECRET: *Put out the welcome mat for your new friends, Obsession and Irrationality. Babies bring out the love and lunacy in all of us.*

Six home pregnancy tests were not enough. I called the 800-number listed on the EPT box and drilled their customer service representative. "When was this test approved by the FDA?" I barked. "What is your false positive rate?"

For eleven years, doctors told me my chances at conception were slim, as scar tissue from a condition called endometriosis accumulated in my abdomen. The odds were further impaired by Duke's work as a naval officer, which kept him away at sea for long stretches. We had made love only one of my supposedly fertile nights during the last month. To top it off, I'd been too tired to hold my legs in the air for forty-five minutes afterward, the trick suggested in a fertility book to propel the swimmers toward the finish line.

A few weeks before, a specialist in San Francisco had put his hand on my shoulder and reassured me outside his Presidio Heights practice. With a Victorian lady nodding in the sun behind him, the doctor said, "You're not going to have any problem. I've seen far worse cases than yours."

Had my body wrapped around the positive thinking that pregnancy was possible? Perhaps inside me there was a little ovum that could. To make it so, a grapefruit-sized fibroid on my one viable ovary had to have shifted ever so slightly to allow an egg to slip into the only tube clear enough of scar tissue to carry it. In turn, the egg had to have met Duke's late-arriving but hearty mates in the nick of baby-making time.

If microcosms could do *that,* I reasoned, medical professionals should be able to get me in for a simple blood test in fewer than three days. But once the blood test was finally dispensed, I wasn't satisfied with the results and stamped my feet until an ultrasound was ordered. I was a woman possessed; I rejected each "congratulations" the pesky Lab Coats offered me.

It hurt inside to hold the reins so tight, but I could not release a decade of pent-up expectation. The ultrasound would certainly show a puffed-up egg trapped in an ovary—a dimly lit dream losing its light amid unmoveable boulders. But on the monitor, fluttering in its sac, hope had attached itself to my uterus. Hope had sent hormones to my head, and a bumpy pox to my breasts. Hope had infiltrated my heart, and science would not let me deny that it was there. At last, I allowed myself to believe the strange and miraculous truth: I was going to be a mother.

The New Gravity

Surprise or planned. Longed for forever or last-minute leap. In utero or in vitro. Adopted or birthed. However you came to the adventure of motherhood, news that you're expecting is so immense that you'll need months and years to take it in. As was true for me and an assortment of round-bellied and child-toting women I've since met, you will likely feel *for a long time* that your perspective on the world has tilted.

From the movies, you know that you're supposed to be serene and all smiles. Yet in reality, your mind is in hyper-drive, trying to settle details of a future you can't truly imagine. Your questions and anxiety often snuff out excitement as you stew. Will the baby be healthy? Will I like being a mom? Will I want to go back to work after the baby comes?, and Will my spouse be as supportive as I need him to be?

The word *numb* comes up a lot among moms when they describe how they felt during pregnancy or their pre-adoption phase. They felt "ecstatic," "lucky," "scared," "overwhelmed," and "purposeful"—all at the same time. A few reveled in being pregnant but most did not adore it.

Feeling a baby kick inside was uniquely exhilarating; having to count her kicks to make sure she was healthy was uniquely nerve-wracking. Looking at an ultrasound or a letter from a Guatemalan orphanage, some moms bonded sight unseen with their children. Others describe the strange sensation of having their pregnant bodies overtaken, seemingly on autopilot, and entirely out of their control.

Your Mortality Is Front and Center

You worry about everything. Unless you were paranoid to start with, obsessing about death and defects is new to you. It seems the minute you decided to have a family, life's subject matter gets far weightier, with fertility and genetic dispositions, miscarriage and preeclampsia representing far bigger threats than an annual job evaluation or being outbid on a home you want to buy.

If you've had a pregnancy end in miscarriage before, the tension is tenfold. The previous pregnancy was so abruptly negated, that you know now how amorphous and vulnerable the idea of "baby" is.

Combine with this the hormonal lenses through which a pregnant mother sees everything and you've got a recipe for w-a-c-k-o. In pregnancy, a woman experiences hormonal fluctuations and corresponding challenges to her emotional health. In this, the most extreme hormonal event a woman will experience, the brain takes hard hits, its biochemistry rattled by surges in estrogen and progesterone, and profound changes in the chemical messages delivered by serotonin, dopamine, and norepinephrine. I won't go into scientific detail, but suffice it to say, these are good drugs, drugs that have a lot to do with your happiness, and the brain is accustomed to a regular fix of them.

Studies reveal that one in ten women experiences symptoms of depression or anxiety during pregnancy, with flare-ups most frequently occurring in the first twelve weeks. Weepiness, irritability, anger, and insomnia often ensue, and women find that their usual abilities to cope and enjoy anticipation of the blessed event are compromised.

Not to mention that doctors tell you virtually any symptom you experience in pregnancy and for years thereafter—from carpal tunnel syndrome to hair loss—is "completely normal." You could have a third eye growing in the middle of your forehead, and an obstetrician would compliment the iris color and tell you "an extra eye is to be expected during pregnancy."

Alicia, a Los Angeles mother of a toddler, read so many articles and manuals about emotional oscillations that two weeks after giving birth, she convinced herself full-blown postpartum depression had set in, when she was only experiencing the milder and more transitory phase called baby blues. But her plight says a lot about first-time mothers: we stand on shaky ground, wondering which gut to trust—the one whose worries are absurd or the one whose worries are important and well-founded.

You Relish the Calm Before the Storm

The summer before my September due date, Duke and I took one last vacation on the island of Martha's Vineyard. My parents joined us for a couple of days, during which time I served as "mistress of pleasing everyone." I'm sure many of you are familiar with this role: making everyone comfortable, seeing to all the details of dinners and clean towels, smoothing out rough edges in conversation, etc.

Exhausted from my vacation, I remember wanting to cling to pregnancy beach and stave off the demands that lay ahead of me in motherhood. Indeed, pregnancy can feel like a beach, a few meters of warm, sparkling sand before you wade into unrelenting surf. Or you may already feel overwhelmed, trying to manage both your pregnancy and the common stresses that hit as couples start families, including the purchase or remodel of a home, the assessment of job satisfaction and income for one or both members of a couple, financial challenges, and/or marital difficulties.

Although you may chide yourself for being unenthusiastic during this splendid passage, psychologists suggest your psyche is girding itself appropriately. Harriet Lerner, Ph.D., the author of *The Mother Dance: How Children Change Your Life,* says there are good reasons to be scared of becoming a mother—for example, of losing too much of your self in motherhood or of seeing your egalitarian marriage divide into two different tracks with the addition of a baby. "When a woman contemplates motherhood, her friends tell her it will change her life. It would be more accurate for them to say, 'You will no longer have what you now call your life. You will have a different life,'" Lerner says.

Welcoming Irrationality into Your World

How do you get yourself ready for this so-called *different* life? Knowing that some of your fears are well grounded, how do you make this wondrous time of expecting a baby less worrisome? How can you conjure some Zen for the formidable journey of birth and new child care to come?

Naturally, your friends and relatives won't let loose with the nitty-gritty at your baby shower. I love a genteel party with cake and punch and presents wrapped in pastel paper. But Indiana Jones–like adventure stories of motherhood might better be shared in dusty, back-alley, Moroccan watering holes. Or, at slumber parties, where expert mommies could rub the swollen ankles of the pledges. In these venues, we could cry, shriek with laughter, and feel the buzz that comes from sharing our reactions to life at its tender, outer edges.

In lieu of that, let's talk about the most pressing pieces of advice, according to my one hundred veteran moms.

Pregnancy, and the Act of Opening your Life Up to Children, Doesn't Breed Rationality

Presumably, up until this point in adulthood, you've been a rational being. You're old enough to know your own mind, and have, by now, probably figured out enough about your monthly cycle to ward off all-night crying jags and full-blown conspiracy theories. Your partner, too, is likely mature and sensible, able to problem-solve and maintain a fairly even keel amid daily stresses.

Stage-left, enter the Tasmanian devil, a twister of estrogen and oxytocin, profound fears, and heartfelt yearnings. To hear a heartbeat on a monitor! To inherit a blanket from your grandmother in which you will soon swaddle your son! This is life-at-its-core stuff, and bound to be staggeringly emotional.

Even physicians confessed to "obsessing" during their pregnancies. By day, Becky (a pregnant primary care doctor in Arizona) and doctors like her take our seemingly neurotic calls, reassuring us that the paint fumes at work or the power lines near the house are harmless to our developing babes. By night, though, Becky was chasing infections, defects, and complications in cyberspace. "I did far more Medline searches than I care to admit." She laughs.

Honestly, what emotions would you expect to accompany the following scenario? You volunteer to gain fifty pounds, embody a nearly two-foot-long human, push it out a small orifice over the course of a day and a half, invite a SWAT team of doctors and nurses into your bedroom, undergo surgery in a last-minute panic, hug a slime-covered creature, and stay up all night pinching your breast into its mouth? The obstacle courses of adoption and surrogacy are just as outlandish. And this is only the first hair-raising passage in the epic of early parenthood.

My friend Kate from our nation's capital is squeamish about slime and gore and asked her doctor if she might forego the scenery of birth by delivering her baby under general anesthesia. When her doctor said no, Kate established some important guidelines for the birth: "I'll be up in first class and there will be a curtain drawn for those of you down in coach. You can bring me a baby wrapped in a pink or blue blanket when you're done."

Indeed, pregnant women—and plebian parents—indulge in many peculiar and obsessive tendencies. Faced with the prospect of losing control of everything we hold dear, we become neurotic about the things we *do* have power over—the way bottles are sterilized, what time baby goes down for his morning nap, or the evil cult of pacifiers and pacifier-pushers.

We love obsessive-compulsives like Jack Nicholson in movies, and quirks in celebrities like Angelina Jolie. But we don't generally admire the same delusions or rants in ourselves. Since parenthood breeds these, I say, let's bring them out of the nursery. Let's turn intense and complicated feelings into a badge of honor, instead of pretending they are deviations from a stern tradition.

Tangled Emotions

In *Middlesex*, the novel by Jeffrey Eugenides about a Greek American family, the narrator is born with both male and female sex characteristics. Nature forces him to contemplate double rather than single truths, but his musings are universally relevant. "Emotions, in my experience, aren't covered by single words. I don't believe in 'sadness,' 'joy,' or 'regret.' Maybe the best proof that language is patriarchal is that it oversimplifies feelings. I'd like to have at my disposal complicated hybrid emotions, German-train car constructions like, say, 'the happiness that attends disaster.'"

How about "the oscillation between joy and sorrow a woman feels while expecting?" Or, "the rage associated with being loving parents of young children?" Unless you're trying to win a June Cleaver lookalike contest, you don't have to censor or suppress your feelings and seemingly out-of-nowhere responses to events that involve your child or child-to-be. Is there any such thing as a reasonable reaction to the first bruise your baby acquires?

The myth of the perfect mother, who only experiences joy, is so pervasive that we think we're not supposed to be conflicted or be-fuddled. But in truth, even if it's well masked, all new moms—and definitely new dads—are a little nuts.

Surround Yourself with People Who Make You Feel Safe

Choosy moms, though, confide their strange new ways of thinking in people who make them feel safe. They are especially choosy when it comes to medical professionals and friends. They also cultivate with spouses *a milieu* in which they don't feel over exposed or vulnerable.

Getting the Bedside Manner You Want

Find doctors and/or midwives who fill pregnancy and childbirth with warm, personal, and communicative encounters. Ask your friends for recommendations. For those of you taking other routes to maternity, nurture a similarly comfortable stance with case workers, attorneys, birth moms, and surrogates.

If you don't feel comfortable with the person who will deliver your baby, consider hiring a doula, a trained coach who can be with you at home and at the hospital throughout labor. (Most doula fees are nominal considering the value they bring, and they often offer sliding scales or payment arrangements.) The doula's job is to calm you and your partner, to help you feel more in control of this im-portant event, and to make sure you, not just the baby, emerge healthfully from the birth experience.

Prepping Spouses and Partners

John Gottman, Ph.D., the nation's premier marriage re-searcher, believes a spouse's empathy with his wife when she becomes a mother is the single most important indicator of their future marital happiness. If your spouse came with the factory-installed level of male sensitivity, he may not grasp the breadth and depth of your feelings on his own.

Weeks before the birth, you may, for example, want to share with him your tremendous fear that he, and a roomful of people, may see you poop a little in the process of pushing the baby out. Once you talk about your discomfort, you may decide he and his seven brothers and sisters should be shooed into the waiting room once the pushing starts.

On the other hand, this talk may be the signal your husband requires to become the champion of your dignity in the delivery room. There, he'll discreetly wipe the poop away, so as to make you feel comforted in the hour you show your most awesome physical power.

Finding Pregnant and Postpartum Confidantes

I learned the hard way how important it is to find mommy confidantes of the same ilk. At a Pampered Chef party full of naval officers' wives, I blurted out to groups of women that early motherhood had shaken me to the core and pushed me close to the brink of madness. The moms I could trust were the ones who yanked me into a corner and started spilling their wine and their guts. The ones who laughed uncomfortably and segued into saying they were born to be mothers, made me cry all the way home, and wake up in the morning wanting to write an exposé about "Mommies Who Lie."

Rather than fall into this trap, start out when you're expecting and share ice cream and inexplicable tears with another pregnant and hormonally deranged friend. It's important to try a couple sound checks in the gulf that sometimes exists between strangers-about-to-be-friends. Try "Check, check, are you disturbed by the amount of goop coming out of your vagina?" Or, "Testing, testing, I sometimes wish this pregnancy was all a crazy dream."

If she doesn't flinch and she can go on to gluttonous enjoyment of her ice cream, make her your regular confidante. It's likely you've found a friend to see you through a million more jubilations and frustrations once your babies come out into the world to play. The two of you can find playgroups that fit your personality, or shun them altogether for your own fellowship.

Stockpile Support and Self-Assurance

I'm not trying to scare you, telling you how much worse parenthood is than you originally thought. Heck, you may turn out to be a baby whisperer. You may have an airtight support network. Or, you may have been visited by one of Dickens's ghosts, seen the real truths of motherhood to come, and are prepared to shift your entire life pace and focus.

But you'd put up the storm shutters if forecasters said a hurricane was likely to hit. As a company manager, you'd prepare yourself and your employees for the repercussions of a hostile takeover, even if the acquiring company ended up being affable. My veteran mommy friends and I suggest you, too, lay in provisions to ease Junior's arrival and your adjustment to the new management of your household.

Lining Up Helpers Galore

First, get help, at least periodic relief, lined-up for six weeks to two months after the birth, not just a week or two. Think about ways to lengthen your husband's paternity leave, keep your mother in town longer, or hire a helper for more time.

Make lists of specific requests such as "Fold laundry," "Bring me fluff magazines," or "Make us a casserole" so you're prepared when people ask you what they can do for you.

Learn to accept every offer of help, even if you tuck away a proffered favor for later. One caveat, though, invite into your home only helpmates with whom you are truly comfortable. Don't be like Pam, a mom in New Jersey who still can't believe she waited on her mother-in-law hand-and-foot for two weeks after giving birth. Don't let your father come with your mom, if he'll end up being helpless and demanding.

Also, be forewarned that you'll likely feel a dollop of competition with those you bring in to help. Your mom's magic touch with babies may feel especially threatening if you're feeling as though you're all thumbs.

Developing a Network of Sitters

It's never too early to start filling a little black book with names and phone numbers of babysitters. Approach this networking task with the zeal you'd apply to gathering contacts in a job search. You'll soon learn which friends hoard sitters and which pals share, but don't rely on their recommendations alone.

Help from professional nanny services, which should be bonded, insured, and do background checks, provide peace-of-mind with a newborn but they cost a bloody fortune. Gyms with child care are a mom's best friend, and many offer classes for post-partum moms in which newborns are allowed to work up a sweat on the sidelines. Child-care providers with whom you arrange day-time care might also babysit at night, or have someone reliable to recommend. Local houses of worship, babysitting certification teachers, child-care facilities and day camps, and principals of parochial or private high schools, to whom the students are well known, can be great resources for finding sitters.

Consider hiring a teenager as a mother's helper during this frazzling time. Not only do you get bright-eyed and inexpensive assistance, you get a chance to orient her and scope out whether she'd be responsible alone with an infant. And don't rule out boy sitters—sons of friends and associates, particularly those who care for their younger brothers and sisters. As is true of my boys with their favorite Saturday night supervisor, Enrique, a great sitter can become an important role model to your child in a relationship that can sometimes be fostered for years.

Amassing Comfort Items

Secondly, stockpile comfort items and sustaining influences. Lots of bottled water will come in handy, as you'll need to keep hydrated if you breast-feed. You'll appreciate having several new, large, and loose cotton T-shirts in flattering colors, because even after giving birth, you probably won't yet fit into pre-pregnancy clothes.

Pick one comprehensive baby health and care guide, maybe two books on breast-feeding if you plan to nurse, and one on getting babies to sleep. Learn only what you need to know now. You're less likely to get overwhelmed and confused if you take things day by day, developmental stage by developmental stage.

Get six favorite CDs, preferably a couple featuring kick-ass women rockers, loaded in your stereo. Buy a "sanity" journal and tuck it and a pen into a side pocket of your glider rocker. Make little reminder signs for the house with sayings like "It takes a village," or "This, too, shall pass." Put into speed-dial friends who can provide great pep talks. And practice little cheers for yourself such as "I'm too sexy for this spittle, too sexy for sterilizing bottles . . ."

Vanquishing Perfectionism

Another calming influence? Lowered expectations. Give your-self permission to eat on paper plates for a year. Commit to spend-ing no more than fifteen minutes on weekdays straightening/cleaning your home. Set a timer, and when the bell goes off, go lie down! Stifle the perfectionist in you long enough to list, together with your spouse, some specific standards you could relax. Priori-tize only your most basic needs.

Trusting Your Gut

Ultimately, the resounding message from the moms I inter-viewed is, do what feels safe and comfortable for you and your fam-ily. Find your truth, follow your heart, and trust your gut. Employ whichever clichéd mantra you need to!

For example, attachment parenting with its co-sleeping empha-sis may be ideal for your friend to raise her baby, but not at all suited to your temperament. Breast-feeding is wonderful and ben-eficial, but it's also incredibly difficult. So go easy on yourself if the adjustment is hard, or you just can't make it work.

A labor and delivery nurse once told me, "There's no right way to have a baby." Likewise, there's also not a single right way to tend an infant or raise a child. Parents, babies, and households are so wildly individual that one-size-fits-all approaches are laughable at best.

You will know your baby best, your marriage best. Even if your own answers seem cockeyed, even if you're tempted to course-correct when you watch other moms, honor your role as the au-thority on making your life-with-a-little-one work.

Remember that your enormous love is at the very crux of all this stress. Then go forward with calm and confidence to meet this new member of your family. Let yourself be as human as the experience itself. Hold the miracle in your hands, and breathe.

What items would *you* include on a baby registry?

"A sign for the front door that reads, 'Baby sleeping; please don't ring bell.'"

"A punching bag for releasing mommy rage."

"A headset for your wireless phone. Hands-free, you can talk on the phone and feed or change a baby."

"A George Foreman grill. Cook lots of chicken at a time so you have ready protein any time."

"A good vibrator, because if you ever feel like having sex again, you want it to be on your own terms."

"Lanolin for sore nipples."

"Herbal sleep aids and teas. When you get the chance to sleep, you want to go down quickly."

"Great-smelling hand and foot lotions. They're an instant pick-me-up when you're feeling demolished."

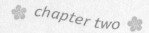 *chapter two*

The Bunk about Birth and Bonding

Learning to Love Your Baby in Your Own Way, On Your Own Terms

> **SECRET:** *Blissed-out bonding is rare; annoyance is common. That's what love is like.*

❀ I gave birth to my second son, Liam, about the same time a very important baby panda was born in our hometown San Diego Zoo. Hua Mei was the first panda born outside of China to survive beyond a few days. Having been artificially inseminated and having carried the cub to term, Bai Yun was hailed by zoologists as being a fabulous mother because she so quickly adapted to the routine of feeding and caring for Hua Mei. Bai Yun stood in stark contrast to a panda mother that had previously rejected her cub, presumably because the baby smelled funny from being handled by a veterinarian right after the birth. The rejection led to the cub's eventual death.

In newspaper stories and twenty-four-hour cub coverage online, I learned the world of panda birth is not that different from our own. We, too, push babies out with a cluster of bystanders rooting for us. We often feel that our inadequacies as new mothers are glaringly visible. Both captive pandas and modern women become parents in a strange environment that is more interested in a baby's well-being than the mother's. And both species face what seem to be pass/fail tests, namely birth and bonding.

Of course I saw myself in the mama panda that walked away. Not that I had rejected my babies by any means, but I was not Bai Yun. She was, after all, the picture of maternal confidence and ease. And most of the time, I felt like a bumbling novice, waiting for the elusive but ever instructive maternal instinct to kick in.

"The Greatest Hour of Earthly Miseries"

As I was, most moms are spoon-fed notions that birth and bonding are exams we have to ace. Then, in the thick of things, we discover that our precious birth plans, outlining our preferences on everything from epidurals to episiotomies, are disposable. And the fabled bonding we're told will come naturally and fill us with goose bumps and life purpose can be thwarted or delayed.

Truth is, the consideration we give birth needs to be amplified and that which we give bonding turned down a notch or two. Most of us underestimate the effects of pulling a live infant from our innards. On the other hand, we expect a wow factor to accompany baby bonding, discounting the experience of moms whose attachments are gradual, slow, or less dramatic.

Our Pilgrim gal-pal predecessors were far more frank, calling childbirth "the greatest hour of earthly miserys" or "the evel hour I look forward to with dread." Of course, women in the seventeenth and eighteenth centuries were sixty-five times more likely to die from complications of birth than women are today. Babies, too, were at tremendous risk, since death in infancy was common and one in ten children died before their fifth birthday.

Today, women are much more apt to discount the birth experience and to think of it as simply a means to a baby-licious end. Because childbirth is now safe, our culture doesn't acknowledge the power of the experience or the fact that few women emerge from it unchanged. That's why, I believe, so many of us are caught off-guard by its tremendous force—physical and psychological.

Today, big-bellied women are encouraged to think of childbirth as beautiful, natural, and happily transformative. Yet the typical labor with a first baby—twelve to fifteen hours long—proves more harrowing than we expect. Despite the bevy of birth stories other moms feel compelled to thrust upon moms-to-be, we all arrive at "ten centimeters and ready to push" in different ways—some of us scared witless, others of us stoic through it all.

In the midst of unprecedented PAIN, many women fear death and dying. Less than a handful of my ensemble of mommy experts encountered a true life-threatening complication while giving birth. Yet, many others *felt* jeopardized because labor pain was startlingly strong or lasting. Or, because a gloved and gowned medical team became alarmed by vital signs they were watching. Moms unsettled by a perceived brush with death or by the naked and nauseating ordeal of labor and delivery don't easily shake these feelings for images of rocking horses and knitted booties.

What If Something Is Wrong with the Baby?

We also fear our babies will have defects or disabilities, only we don't readily admit to these fears. Tensions intensify for us as contractions do, so that until the swaddled one is delivered pink and perfect, with healthy Apgar scores, we don't realize the burdensome fright we've been hauling around. Many moms said their tears in the delivery room were not so much tears of joy but those of immense relief.

In the days of hoop skirts and bloomers, American women gave birth at home with a midwife attending, and a group of female relatives and neighbors at her bedside to offer encouragement, support, and undoubtedly a nip of something straight from the jug. They got an enormous smorgasbord feast afterwards, too.

Medical monitoring and interventions are the big players in today's hospital births, relegating support and encouragement to minor-league roles. Often, we feel that doctors and nurses hold all the cards and that the small amount of control we have is expressed in our birth plans. Yet, when our bags of water break, we discover that our birth plans might as well have been shredded into confetti and dropped from the ceiling of the LDR, or labor/delivery/recovery room.

Bye, Bye Birth Plan

Sometimes birth plans are tossed because we get sixteen hours into the contractions, into panic and excruciating pain, and all we want is *for it to be over*. Mostly though, plans change because medical teams avert all possible, though not very probable, risks. So, for example, women in labor spend less time walking, which often speeds the opening of the cervix, and more time in bed, tied to monitors of the baby's heartbeat, than is probably necessary.

Bitterness about decisions that took you away from your desired birth can leave a bad taste with you for days and weeks afterwards. Too many women see birth as a kind of "test" and are stung by a sense of failure if they accept anesthesia when they hadn't intended to or are unable to deliver the baby vaginally. Self-imposed or coached into this mind-set, moms nevertheless can carry around for weeks afterward the feeling that their bodies or their doctors betrayed them. It's a bigger feeling, and harder to put down, than you might expect.

Birth's Emotional Side Effects

One Connecticut mom I know cut her family off from touching or holding her newborn almost immediately after birth. So shaken was she by dips in the baby's heart rate during delivery that she carried fear of his death to an extreme, not letting him out of her sight. Weeks of bed rest she'd endured so as not to endanger her baby before his birth also seemed to have taken their toll, her sense of life's fragility now on high alert.

The day women give birth, we experience as much as a one thousand-fold drop in hormonal levels. Most of us are ill-prepared for the emotional consequences this hormonal bungee can cause.

Dee Nipper, a doula for twenty years in San Diego, says the birth experience opens everything up—floodgates of emotions with regard to your sexuality, your sense of control and power, even your childhood. For this reason birth can in a small percentage of women be truly traumatic, leaving behind symptoms of post-traumatic stress disorder. For the remainder of us, the opening floodgates and chemistry experiments going in our bodies produce results no one warned us about: emotions more profound and permanent than we were warned to expect in the mild "baby blues."

The Bunk About Bonding

With stitches in the perineum and hemorrhoids rampant, postpartum moms have enough to worry about. But two Australian chaps inadvertently gave new mothers another hurdle. Researchers Marshall Klaus and John Kennell coined the term *bonding* in the 1970s to describe a phenomenon in which mothers who had skin-to-skin contact with their babies 30–60 minutes after birth experienced a "specially sensitive state which made them unusually ready to 'fall in love' with their child."

Subsequent research has not confirmed the physiologic state Klaus and Kennell described. Yet, we know that touching and massaging a newborn stimulates breathing, that a mother's heartbeat can quiet an infant used to the uterine environment, and nipple contact stimulates the release of oxytocin, the so-called "cuddle hormone" that helps contract the uterus and inhibit bleeding. Undoubtedly, there is a synchronized dance of physiology that takes place in a mom's and baby's reactions to one another.

Bonding is a trust built between a needy baby and a responsive caretaker, over repetition of "crying" and "soothing" episodes. Somehow though, "bonding" became an all-encompassing term, the buzz word for the entire relationship between mother and child. We use the term to describe an ethereal connection we feel with our young, evidence of the maternal instinct at work. This little cocktail of bonding and instinct makes "the perfect mother."

Bonding with a Capital "B"

Bonding becomes too big for its britches when it's used inter-changeably with "attachment," a broader scientific term that describes the affection between a child and his caretaker that propels him to healthy, emotionally balanced adulthood. Although attachment difficulties are most commonly identified in adoption and foster care systems, the reason many moms quit jobs and stay at home—and many more fret that they can't—is to establish connections during the first eighteen months of a child's life that they believe will be of lifelong value.

Yet, as Carin Rubenstein notes in her book *The Sacrificial Mother: Escaping the Trap of Self-Denial,* psychology's dirty little secret is that there is no real proof this early and all-important connection exists. Even if it does exist, science hasn't shown that this connection has anything to do with how well-adjusted or sociable a child is later in life.

Indeed, we know that genes have the greatest influence over a child's future personality. Social circumstances also have an impact, such as being born and growing up poor, or experiencing a frequent number of divorces or moves during childhood. Contrary to what many of us believe about the decisive influence of the parent-infant relationship, studies of identical twins who were adopted at birth and raised by different mothers and fathers demonstrate that no matter who raises them, identical twins grow up to be uncannily similar.

Am I Bonding Correctly?

The moms I know are terribly confused and have very different definitions of bonding. Some moms meant it literally, as in the "immediate inclination to mother." A good portion of moms felt this sensation even while they were pregnant, perhaps fueling their nesting instinct. Other moms felt a profound bond when they first held their babies and said it seemed as if they were "born to do this."

Others, though, felt bonding was a decision—that at some point they consciously chose to let themselves fall head over heels for the wrinkled bundle in their arms. And a couple of moms believed that bonding was a hoax. They didn't accept it as a postpartum milestone, much less a litmus test of good mothering.

Despite our varied definitions, many of us expect baby love and the ability to mother to arise from the mist, in the same romantic way described in *InStyle* and other magazines' celebrity mom profiles. Jane Seymour, Reese Witherspoon, Christie Brinkley, and Jada Pinkett Smith welcomed us into their Malibu mansions and Hamptons hideaways to see how babies had met their deepest yearnings for happiness. As mommies, they were thin and radiant in nurseries with hand-painted murals or at catered showers attended by Hollywood's glitterati of childbearing years. Literally and figuratively, they shared recipes so we could be just like them, only without a staff of nannies, personal chefs, and trainers.

Logically then, in our postpartum haze, we wonder where our expected bliss has gone. We fail to recognize what psychiatrists know very well: Many people initially respond to intense feelings by distancing themselves.

If our bliss is mitigated by fear, or goes underground while we sort out the enormity of love we feel, we think we don't have the right stuff for motherhood. We worry, can our babies tell that our whole hearts are sometimes not in it? And, if we hold our infants and toddlers close but don't experience a giddy tingle inside, does it mean bonding is doomed?

Stop the Madness!

Before you start tallying your missteps and inadequacies in early motherhood, take some advice from my learned friends and me. Nearly all of us have had moments when we doubted we were cut out for parenthood. We feel an abiding love for our kids. We see before us babies that thrive and grow, smile and walk. Yet, that isn't enough. We still harangue ourselves for not being the mothers we feel our natural instincts are supposed to produce.

To stop the flogging, and settle our nervous hearts, we're learning to repeat out loud the following truths.

Fall in Love at Your Own Pace and Tempo

My 50-year-old friend Lisa, an author in Chicago, recalls holding her baby son, Luke, for the first time: "I simply could not believe it. There are no words for it. I was viscerally in love. His skin, his smell—he was perfection."

To this day, Lisa is smitten, now staring at seven-year-old Luke on the subway. "He's so beautiful to me, I am so proud of him. It's a joy to look at him and see this blend of us—his father and me. My worry is that I care too much. I've never had to pump myself up to do more for him. It's always been all-out."

Love at first sight, in courtships and with babies, is our romantic ideal. We expect to coo the way Lisa did, with all-out reverence. And indeed, more than half of the women I interviewed reported bonding "immediately."

Yet, there are other wonderful, quirky ways that moms and dads develop connections with their babies, none of them reflective of parenting gone wrong.

Julia from Cincinnati bonded differently with each of her two children. "The second I saw my son, my first thought was 'I was meant to be this child's mommy. This is what I was put on earth to do.'" With her second child, a daughter, Julia says, "I didn't really bond until she and I went to my ten-year college reunion. She was nine months old! I think it was the first time I didn't feel guilty paying more attention to her than to my son. And I know it was the first time I began to appreciate her unique qualities."

Gayle, a thirty-eight-year-old mom who lives in the Berkshires of Massachusetts, says that childbirth, seventeen hours long, was one of the worst experiences of her life. "It was physically traumatic, scary, and overwhelming." She threw up frequently, got the shakes, and "had no sense of the outside world" for hours on end.

After Bethany was born, Gayle just wanted to be mothered, and to "lick the wounds of delivery." People did not "see the injury I was experiencing, or comfort me." Friends who visited kept saying to her, "You must be so happy!" "I kept thinking to myself, 'Why would I be?!'"

The first night, Gayle sent Bethany to the hospital's newborn nursery—something she now regrets. "I was too afraid," she says. With the reality of being a mother setting in, Gayle explains, "I was trying to delay the onset of my new job."

Within a few weeks though, when the baby gained weight and Gayle felt as though her parts were working again, she "relaxed and let the bonding happen." Then, Gayle abandoned plans to use part-time daycare because she couldn't imagine leaving Bethany. "I love being with her. The few times I have gone out alone, I drive away and feel that something's missing."

In other nations and cultures, moms get help so that they can bond well and get their postpartum needs met. In Malaysian villages for example, Mom and baby do not rejoin the community for forty days. During this reprieve, mothers receive hot baths infused with fragrant leaves. They are massaged from head to toe with herbs, with special attention paid to rubbing the abdomen to shrink the uterus.

"Where's my herbal massage?" you may be asking. Well, as much as bonding is endorsed in this country, American moms contend with rushed hospitalizations, and nursing ratios that often cannot accommodate breaks for mom to sleep or take time off from baby care. We face the additional healing required by an unusually high C-section rate, and don't automatically receive home visits from a doula or baby nurse as mothers in European nations do.

All Moms Bumble

In the crucial first two weeks after I gave birth to my son Patrick, our pediatrician told us the baby was not "thriving." First, Patrick had to be re-hospitalized for treatment for jaundice and spent hours under therapeutic lights that kept me from holding or nursing him. My milk was slow to come in and then I never seemed to produce enough. Patrick's doctor urged Duke and me to supplement my breast milk with formula.

On the contrary, lactation specialists I consulted were adamant that a bottle could bring on "nipple confusion," in which the baby begins to prefer bottle-fed formula over the breast. They recommended I pump milk between each feeding, which meant that every two hours, after letting Patrick nurse for forty minutes on each side, I let a grinding mechanism manipulate my breasts for a half hour and got a whopping ten minutes off before starting the feeding routine all over again.

Eventually, I sent all boob-obsessed parties to their corners and devoted myself to what I called "bovine therapy"—constant and unremitting feeding of the little skeleton boy, who could seemingly suck the life out of me. I did so, lying down in bed, where I could sleep and Patrick could gnaw and suck at will.

My milk production did increase, and a few weeks later we added a bottle of formula in the afternoons when I was particularly depleted. Patrick grew one chin after another, we both survived, and are now as tight as thieves.

All of us hit potholes in our bonding journey. Yet, unlike any other endeavor we undertake in our lives, we believe that from the start we have to be perfect at parenting. We expect to be naturally endowed with knowledge and ability, or to augment our skill with help from a plethora of child-care manuals. No learning curve is permitted.

We can't afford a learning curve, you see, because the latest research maintains the most critical period of brain cell firing occurs in the first three years of life. To ensure optimal health and intellect, we have to hold a baby so many hours, respond to her cries within so many seconds, and talk to her whenever she's awake—preferably in several languages. We resist pacifiers for this reason, and bottles in bed for another. Dad can't be too entrenched in work that he fails to provide the appropriate proportion of male modeling. Mom can't work at all, lest she doom her child to daycare, patterns of aggressive behavior, and substandard intellectual stimulation. In this context, it's a wonder any of us escape the pressure with our panda esteem in tact.

Sometimes it simply takes settling into your own skin again to allow bonding to occur. A year and a half after Patrick was born, Duke and I escaped to Palm Springs for our first weekend away from our little dictator. At an outdoor café, I kept remarking how incredible the sun felt and how delicious the food tasted. Even my otherwise dormant sexuality was revived over this break.

So it was that in a shower at an inn an hour's distance from my baby and home, I bonded with my firstborn. You see, for hours by the pool that day, I'd consumed Anna Quindlen's *Black and Blue* about a mother and her little boy's escape from an abusive spouse. At its devastating conclusion, when the main character loses her son to his terrible father, I started to cry. But it wasn't until I was under the shower nozzle that the wailing began and that I realized the truth: I had never been more vulnerable, never more susceptible to devastation, than in this moment, when I realized how completely I loved and was devoted to Patrick. The notion of losing him, jarred loose in me by Quindlen's book and a relaxing weekend, showed me how *attached* I really was.

Bond Your Own Way

How much better off *you* will be, understanding that some moms are infatuated from day one and some moms find love bowls them over in a fit of tears months later. The same is true with dads, though research tells us men typically follow a year behind moms in their emotional adjustment to parenthood. It's common for fathers to lag behind in the bonding process.

All this said, take heart. Because it really *does not matter* how you or your spouse come to feel affection for your child. It only matters that you do.

Give in to Skin-to-Skin

One of the secrets moms are too self-conscious to share is how exquisite it is to cuddle with their babies and children. We don't talk about the "sensuality" of the mother/child relationship for fear of people thinking we mean "sexuality." Yet, there are few more intoxicating pleasures in life than falling asleep with your baby in your arms, carrying a snoozing toddler to his bed, or holding hands with your son on the way to the bus stop.

The sheer physicality of motherhood is staggering. You are, most often, the body the babe craves, the one associated with food and comfort, and later the *only* one capable of chasing away nightmares. Infants crave us because they know our scents, recognize our voices from the womb, or get accustomed to us as their primary caregivers.

But the intensity of a baby's desire can be overwhelming and frightening. It blows apart feminist theory such as "Men and women can do the same job equally well." It makes you question the Creator, "Did you design us this way so we would be encumbered with children and unable to do ANYTHING else?" It makes all the dreams you had of maintaining your life, outside of motherhood, seem like a chalk drawing, pelted by rain.

No More Personal Space
This pressing body stuff is alarming for parents who need privacy or are uncomfortable with intimacy. When my sister, Catherine, had her first son, Taylor, I remember watching her carefully shore up her boundaries. She pumped milk but did not breast-feed directly. Taylor slept in his room from the first night home on. She cautioned friends not to cradle her slumbering boy for long, lest he grow to depend on being held.

Catherine adored her son and worried about doing the right things for him. But she wasn't willing to have Taylor impede on her long-held realm of modesty, even if it would make her life, managing a new baby, easier.

I saw the fears of Every Mom being played out in Catherine's home. The first weeks postpartum, the lines between you and baby are terribly blurred. Where you stop and the baby begins is unclear.

It's natural to resist the cloying nature of these interactions, and to sink a flag into dominions you want to remain your own.

Touch Simply Works

Yet, there are two compelling reasons for softening your position, as Catherine discovered and went on to implement with her second baby. One, infants and children respond to touch. Letting little Russell into your bed may very well mean that you get all-important REM sleep. Carrying Chloe in a Snugli® may mean dinner gets prepared and you and your husband aren't wigged out during those stressful evening hours. In other words, by allowing the baby into your personal space, you may gain more sanity than you surrender.

Secondly, if you give in to skin-to-skin to any degree, you'll experience the loveliest, and I would say holiest, aspects of parenting. Indeed, more than half of the women I interviewed said their most contented moments of motherhood occurred when they were snuggling with their kids. Seeing your husband skin-to-skin, tiny fingers resting on a wide chest, is spine-tingling, too.

Kim, the mother of three in Maryland, says she loves to rub her children's hair and heads. Never again will Kim resist a head rub from *her* mom, now that she knows how immensely full of love and delight that gesture is.

Kisses on the Lips

Another mom was embarrassed to admit that she likes when her kids kiss her on the mouth. If you didn't grow up in a demonstrative Italian or Greek family, or even if you did, you may of late have reserved kisses on the lips for romantic life. Then the closeness of family calls out to be expressed, and your lips become healing to boo-boos and pink targets for little puckered mouths that want to tell you they love you.

When I was first married I was amazed that my husband's first impulse, even before consciousness in the morning, was to reach for me. Now my four-year-old, Liam, cannot start the day without making body contact. Though I can't sleep while spooning with my husband, Liam and I meld in these perfectly comfortable ways. If his face is not touching mine, he sleepily shifts to make it so. And even his morning breath is sweet-smelling to me in this predawn sanctuary of mom and child.

Later in the day, Liam will get up on my lap and lift his T-shirt and mine to expose our stomachs so we sit together, skin to skin. In this incredibly literal way, he reminds me that we once shared my belly, and that I will always be the origin of love for him.

This proximity was so off-putting and scary in the beginning. Now, between preschool and soccer practice, dinner preparation and homework, I just can't get enough.

Strangely, by surrendering boundaries and adopting a language of touch, you discover your uncanny, innate power for healing, molding, and emboldening your young. Cheek to cheek, hand to tummy, or warm feet to Popsicle toes with your little one, you will feel a connection to mothers and sons/mothers and daughters the planet through.

Once you get comfortable with the closeness, I guarantee you will be addicted, too. Any anxieties you have over bumbling the bonding process can be healed with hugs and more hugs.

A Delay in Bonding Is Not Harmful

Moms are prevented from immediate, full-fledged bonding for all sorts of reasons. Try forging natural connections when you've been released from the hospital and only get to visit your preemie in a neonatal intensive care unit. Parents who've endured arduous fertility treatments, or those who elected to terminate a previous pregnancy due to birth defects, sometimes have trouble adjusting to a happy outcome.

Krista of Savannah, Georgia, is a thirty-seven-year old adoptive mother who didn't truly connect with her son for about six months. "In large part," Krista says, "I didn't bond right away because I was overwhelmed by gratitude toward his birthmother, and guilty that I was better prepared to raise him than she was." Nothing written about bonding can prepare moms for feelings such as Krista's, which are complex and not easily whisked away, even in the presence of a miracle baby.

Postpartum Depression and Adjustment Disorders

The United States has the highest rate of postpartum depression of any industrialized country. While hormones play a major part, postpartum depression is an equal opportunity troublemaker, as one set of gay parents recently told me.

My neighbor John and his partner, Jason, became parents by adopting a child born to a surrogate. They saw the surrogate mom through a first pregnancy that ended in miscarriage, and a second she carried to full-term, to bring home gorgeous Anna with the dark brown curls. Yet, the first weeks with Anna—in which they rarely slept, went out, or did anything but figure out how to get Anna to sleep—plunged John into a clear-cut case of postpartum melancholy.

John describes his long, fretful nights "I paced the hallway at night, thinking to myself, 'Oprah will have me on her show. I will be the first person ever to have paid $80,000 for a baby, and gone through all the difficulties of adopting as a gay couple with a surrogate, only to have given my baby up for adoption in the first month.'"

If you think new moms are isolated, try being a new gay dad, John says. "None of my friends could relate at all to what Jason and I were going through with Anna. We were at totally different points in our lives."

Indeed, the enormous life adjustments that babies bring can contribute to earthquakes within. Increasingly, psychiatrists report, new moms and dads are being diagnosed with "adjustment disorders"— disruptions in mental and emotional health that occur when these budding parents try to absorb this jolting life change. And if you're struggling to find your equilibrium in this new life and your biology is also out of whack, your ability to meet all the needs of your newborn can be dramatically impaired.

Six days into motherhood, after an uncomplicated C-section, Teresa, a school psychologist in Houston, developed difficulties breathing and a quickened heart rate. At first her doctor suspected a pulmonary embolism, which occurs in rare instances after birth, but it turned out postpartum panic attacks were the culprit.

Yet, a subsequent Zoloft prescription from her primary care doctor—to tide her over till she could see a psychiatrist—contributed to a "downward tail spin." Two weeks into the treatment, Teresa says, "I couldn't function, I had insomnia. I was terribly anxious and mildly depressed. I was hiding in corners of a room, thinking I wanted to drive off a bridge."

Fortunately, Teresa could hand Taylor off to her mother, who moved in and lived with Teresa's family for two and a half months. The expert on postpartum anxiety and depression with whom she met changed the medications and gave her small doses of narcotics that enabled her to sleep. "I could literally feel the stabilization of my body," Teresa says. "I learned that my body could not withstand the incredible hormonal drop that comes with childbirth. In my case, the problem was 99 percent biochemical. Nowhere in the dozens of books I had read was there a description of the magnitude of these side effects."

Eschewing breast-feeding, which she had planned to do, Teresa started taking birth control pills again, which restored her estrogen, a hormone often tied to happiness in women. Teresa actually welcomed her first period, saying, "I felt I was finally in my own body again."

Counseling was also helpful. "I was immediately reassured by my psychiatrist that I was experiencing a time-limited illness, and

Fact and Fiction about Birth and Babies

Misnomer

My doctor/midwife and I will follow my birth plan. · · · · · · · · · · · · ·

My stomach will shrink right after birth. · · · · · · · · · · · · · · · · ·

Contractions stop once the baby is born. · · · · · · · · · · · · · · · ·

I'm eager to share the baby with friends and family. · · · · · · · · · ·

Baby blues last only a few days. ·

Breast-feeding is the only choice. ·

Dad can share the work. ·

I can work from home during my maternity leave. · · · · · · · · · · ·

I'll get up at night; my husband is working. · · · · · · · · · · · · · · ·

How hard can parenting be? Everyone does it. · · · · · · · · · · · · ·

that my baby would get the love and care she needed from my mother in the meantime."

Are You At Risk?

Remember, you may be at higher risk for postpartum depression if you or members of your family have experienced depression; if you have a difficult labor and delivery or a C-section; if you are adopted; if you have had an abortion or miscarriage in the past; or if you are a victim of rape or incest.

The important message here is that whether or not you suffer

Real Truth

- Birth went somewhat diferently than we expected.
- You'll likely wear maternity clothes for weeks after birth.
- Contractions continue for a while after birth.
- Limit visitors. I need my rest.
- You may feel sad and overwhelmed for months.
- Breast-feeding is very tough; it doesn't work for everyone.
- Dad can share some tasks but babies mostly want Mom.
- I should never have said I would work during my leave.
- Resentment of spouse who sleeps often develops.
- Parenthood is the hardest job I'll ever have.

from postpartum depression—from "baby blues," the mild sadness and anxiety that comes a few days after birth, to a more serious form—your health and well-being cannot be denied. Attend to your needs as best you can and stop worrying about bonding. Dads, partners, grandparents, and friends can satisfy and comfort babies until storms calm for Mom and illness remits.

Nothing in the baby literature tells moms that sometimes, it's all right to put ourselves first or that often a baby's health depends on Mommy attending to her own health. A mom, who was both a homemaker and pilot's wife, once sat across a café table from me and whispered that it was okay to let a baby cry, for hours at a time, if it came to that. "When my husband was away, and I had no help for days on end with a toddler and a newborn, I learned that sometimes, I had to put myself first. I could not stay up all night every night, soothing an inconsolable baby. Sometimes I had to put my own health before hers so I would turn off the monitor and go to sleep. It was the scariest, most radical thing I'd ever done. And no one but my husband ever told me it was all right to do that. So now, I tell every new mother I know."

Amid bumbling and delays, babies can and do bond, despite the fact that moms are human and have needs, too. Corny as it sounds, Teresa says postpartum depression was "the best, and the worst, thing that ever happened to me. Of course it has made me more sympathetic in my work. But it also totally changed my outlook on parenthood, so that now I don't sweat the small stuff. I see my girlfriends killing themselves trying to maintain order in their homes, and I think, 'Just sit down in the mess and enjoy your baby.'"

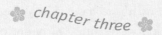 *chapter three* ❀

I'm Deprived, Verging on Deranged

Conquering the First Rocky Months of Motherhood

> **SECRET:** *A new mom's spirits are not necessarily bright. Lighten up. Know that you're normal, and that "wonder babies" are a farce.*

❀ It was Tuesday mid-morning, although weekdays were indistinguishable from weekends when Patrick was eight months old. I had bronchitis, and my whole body hurt when I coughed. Patrick had an ear infection, and all he wanted to do was nurse and doze in my arms, shedding tears (which didn't accompany his usual cries) when I put him in his crib. The antibiotics he was getting, both from his medicine and mine via breast milk, had given him nonstop, gushing diarrhea. Then despite changing him and cleaning his bottom constantly, he developed a terrible rash, bright red and bumpy, so that he howled when I applied ointment.

The baby care books said to let him go without a diaper for a while. So I sat in our den, with towels draped over the couch and me, his sore bottom exposed, his mouth on my breast, and cough drops for Mommy on my left. Then his penis sent a giant arch of urine across the room onto the TV screen. And simultaneously he soaked the towel in my lap with dirt-colored liquid. With Patrick still nursing, and a coughing attack coming on, I tried rolling the towels up on my lap with one hand. Lucky, our dog, barked and scratched at the back door, wanting to be let in. Then my editor called, the one I talked to only after rehearsing jokes in front of the mirror, or crafting conversation starters on notepads.

Fortunately, neither she nor I remember what was said, as I improvised, liquid poop all over me. But once we hung up, a single friend from Boston called, to whom I tearfully confessed my status quo. Dear Beth—former drinking companion in college, now aunt to several—encouraged me to get in the bathtub with baby Patrick, where both of us could get clean, and upholstery could be temporarily spared.

In the bathtub, life got simpler and sweeter. The baby giggled through his first bath with Mom, breast-fed and splashed at will, and immersed his chafing hips in a sitz bath. The phone rang, the dog barked, but we were relaxed and clean, readying ourselves for a long afternoon's nap together.

Marvels and Meltdowns

The early months of motherhood are treacherous, full of marvels but also full of meltdowns. At some point, it's quite likely that frustration and bleary-eyed exhaustion will press you to question why you wanted children in the first place. Believe me, this is a normal part of the initiation process.

Sure, in the hours after giving birth, you and baby have warm, satin-finished, pink and coral tones that make you "glow." But subsequently you'll also have your share of cheeks blotchy from tears or cheeks overtaken by the red of rage or frustration.

Libby from Bangor, Maine, who gave birth to a daughter six months ago, recollects the day she and her husband brought their newborn home from the hospital. "I've never felt so incompetent in my life. No maternal instinct kicked in. In fact, I stood there at the threshold thinking, What the hell do we do with her now?" In this disorienting time, she says, "It's too much to ask that moms also be happy."

"Baby People"

Of course, some moms are blessed with knowing exactly what to do at this threshold because they are "baby people." My author friend Lisa, the one who bonded on sight, also made being a new—and single—mother look remarkably easy. She finished writing a novel the first year of Luke's life, and carried on a transcontinental romance that took her and the baby to the Wailing Wall in Israel and to castles in Scotland. Flight attendants taught her the term *broody* to describe people like her who were magnetically drawn to infants and children.

"The baby stage was incredible," Lisa says ecstatically. "I loved being the only thing he wanted. All you have to do with babies is love them. Toni Morrison said that a baby's greatest need is for you to be the person you really are, which I think is so true. When I was his whole world, I could, ultimately, be myself."

Yet, Dalia—a mother in Denver of two children under the age of five—found the baby stage torturous. For the first year of her daughter's life, Dalia says, "I didn't feel very connected to Elizabeth. I was terribly bored. I experienced a lot of extremes—happy one minute, sad the next. And it seemed as though my head was not on straight."

Inherent in the baby routine is the need to be at home to get Baby and Mom down for naps, but the longer Elizabeth fussed and refused to sleep, the more time Dalia spent isolated and alone. A community activist accustomed to a high visibility full-time job and a large social circle, Dalia could not draw on her usual sources of happiness. Only when Elizabeth grew older and they were able to get out for lunch or meet friends at the park, did Dalia regain more of her equilibrium. "My friends and their war stories about motherhood are my saving grace," Dalia says.

The baby stage has some distinct advantages including frequent naps and docile periods in which you can be otherwise engaged; reduced expectations on parents; and transportability of a baby to restaurants, movies, and gatherings that may not be toddler-friendly. But babies who don't latch well or alternatively never take to a bottle, who don't sleep or wail unendingly, and those who are easily overstimulated make the first year an extremely stressful period to survive. You want to be one of those people with the perfect babies, and resent the suggestion that calm babies are the product of "good" mothers.

Get Ready to Regress

Prior to our quest to have families, most of us moms were headstrong women in a Western world that prizes independence, self-sufficiency, mastery, productivity, efficiency, and money. Ask a woman what she liked best about herself before she became a wife and mother and you're likely to hear: "I was on my own and made my own way in the world," "I was admired for my work," "I depended on myself for almost everything," or "I was free to pounce on opportunities."

Then plop this independent gal into motherhood and see how she flails. The masculine traits that served women well in career and life immediately clash with the requirements of mothering.

In *Women's Moods: What Every Woman Must Know about Hormones, the Brain, and Emotional Health*, Deborah Sichel, M.D., and Jeanne Watson Driscoll, M.S., R.N., C.S., say it well: "The postpartum period is an inherently regressive time, when a woman needs to depend on others for care, food and safety. She must be able to relinquish her assertive role and allow others to care for her so she is freed to care for her baby."

Indeed, this is a tall order. Drop that recordbreaking efficiency and your down-to-a-science multi-tasking, because your maximum speed will now be a snail-paced ten miles per hour. You must focus on each infinitesimally tiny miracle of your baby's first months and be present "in the moment," not distracted by the fourteen other tasks you're used to simultaneously managing. For the next year, you will accomplish absolutely nothing except for feeding and diapering. And, despite your usual comprehensive research and thoughtful planning, your child will prove so unpredictable that feeling good about your work, much less that you're on top of it, is out of the question.

In business jargon, Western moms go into parenting with an entirely different "skill set" than that which the job requires. Legend has it we're endowed with the right stuff for motherhood, except that most of us are rusty, having spent the last decade or two working in other arenas than babysitting. The adjustment is so abrupt and so dramatic that it paralyzes many moms, with the exception of a few women I met who had remained especially close to their extended families. These moms had realistic expectations of life with small children because of their longtime exposure to the little menaces.

Why Am I Not Better at This?

Others of us, who expect to conquer motherhood the same way we did the work world or single life, end up asking one painful question: "What the hell is wrong with me?"

Janine, a former elementary school teacher in Oregon, asked this, too. For the first four months of his life, Janine's newborn wailed incessantly from 8:30 A.M. to 5 P.M. every day. She remarks, "When my husband got home from work, he'd get the baby down for a nap very easily, and say to me, 'What's the problem?' And, for weeks, I kept taking the baby to the doctor but they told me the crying was nothing to worry about."

Janine continued, "There was nothing else I could do but hold the baby, try to calm him, and try to calm myself. Meanwhile my three-year-old son watched TV ten hours a day." When she said this, Janine broke down in tears, guilt-ridden about neglecting her oldest.

Janine's littlest one turned out to have a milk allergy, a problem that was easily solved. Once relieved, the baby got much easier to handle, and Janine stopped blaming herself for the enormous strain her family experienced.

A baby's cry pushes an adult's blood pressure up and quickens his or her heart rate, sometimes steeply. Imagine weeks on end in which nervous tension wore at Janine, her baby's screams keeping her shoulders tight to her neck, the pacing and rhythmic jiggling meant to soothe her newborn also making her back and arms ache and the muscles spasm. Then affix a displaced preschooler who wants Mommy to himself, a husband who isn't very empathetic, medical professionals who tell her nothing is wrong, and a claus-trophobic house isolating mom from the healing empathy and support she needs. You've got all the ingredients of a deranged, deprived new mommy—someone who loves her family so much that she'll suffer and blame herself for the stresses at hand.

I Don't Recognize My Own Body

Compounding problems, few women realize their bodies will not, and may never be, the same after giving birth. I have the misfortune of permanently retaining a pregnant woman's uncanny sense of smell. Five years after giving birth, a whiff of the bathrooms I share with three males at home—despite frequent cleaning—evokes the aroma of subway stations in most major cities.

Postpartum body changes exceed saggy breasts, rolls of extra stomach skin, or a bigger shoe size. The extreme hair loss a few months after childbirth is maddening. And as sick as you may be of maternity clothes, you may not fit into anything else for some weeks after birth. Over the long term, many moms will be plagued with weight problems and the loss of self-esteem larger sizes can bring.

"I was so excited when I heard that as a new mom, I wouldn't have time to eat," laughs a Las Vegas mother of a six-month-old boy struggling to lose fifteen post-childbirth pounds. "But like all the other phases in life in which I was supposed to be too nervous or too busy to eat, I ate right through it."

As if it hasn't wreaked enough havoc, sleep deprivation also boosts the production of cortisol, a stress hormone that regulates your metabolism of sugar, protein, and fat. Excess cortisol also sends insulin levels soaring, which control blood sugar and fat storage, so that weight loss is more difficult.

Another disappointment? Breast-feeding does not always peel

off pounds; sometimes, moms don't shed extra weight till they finish nursing. Other moms can't slim down till they have dedicated hours in which to exercise, hours that are hard to come by during the preschool years.

Am I Dumber Than I Used to Be?

Our brains are not exactly razor sharp in the new mommy stage. Recent findings demonstrate that diminished mental acuity and memory are side effects during, and for several years after, pregnancy. Night after night of interrupted sleep, in which we never achieve the recuperative stage of the rapid eye movement or REM sleep, also make us slow-moving. As more and more mothers of young children continue paid work, our mental function may also be discombobulated by needing to have our heads in two places at once. We mostly say "mommy brain" in jest, but the phenomenon is real: we're not our usual sharp-minded selves.

On Patrick's first visit to my native Kansas City when he was nine months old, my high school friend and I decided enough with Baby van Gogh, it was time for the real thing: a trip to the Nelson Art Gallery. The first setback was a security guard's firm reproach of my baby backpack so that I would quickly develop worn-out arms in addition to museum feet.

Then, after seeing three paintings, tops, Patrick made his chow requirements known, and Diane found a lunch table for us in a lovely fountain-filled courtyard. I remember composing a sentence, getting three words in, readjusting my son so he was comfortable, then realizing I was exposing my breast to the entire metropolitan area. I utterly forgot what I'd been trying to say. Conversation, if you can call it that, went on this way for seven or more disjointed thoughts, before Diane and I settled for quiet admiration of the beautiful room and the mixed greens on our plates. I remember thinking I would never make cogent dialogue again.

Over the long run, though, the ways in which motherhood messes with our brains turns out to be good. Artists with bulging tummies or nursing newborns notice ideas come to them more easily, and that inspiration abounds. A few years into parenthood, moms also become more efficient, and their practice at juggling enormous responsibilities pays off in the end.

Exciting new research studies demonstrate that mothers' brains actually grow, because we're exposed to such enormous new challenges and complexities, and acquire many new talents and skills as a result. The studies suggest that the ways in which our mommy brains stretch, grow, and fire new synapses are eventually a windfall for us. We become bolder, braver, and more efficient in the wake of early motherhood.

Before that recovery occurs, however, many moms feel that a tectonic plate has shifted beneath them. The pressures on mothers have never been more intense, the emotional earthquakes among us never stronger or more numerous. As of yet, only a cadre of medical professionals—often women doctors who have experienced the adjustment themselves—acknowledge the increasing numbers of angry and utterly depleted new mommies. Indeed, the medical community is not yet addressing the fact that postpartum depression and anxiety are the biggest complications of modern birth.

Fault Lines

We are all vulnerable to eruptions, when our bodies experience normal but radical hormonal changes and are assaulted with the stress early parenthood can bring. Most of us already have fault lines running through us. A fault line may emerge when you experience a heartbreak or tragedy that you never adequately mourn. It may occur because your brain is overtaxed by a relentless bombardment of information, or because your body so rarely burns off the stress response daily life triggers in you.

You may have pre-existing fault lines, too. Say, if anyone in your family has suffered with depression or anxiety. Or if, when you first got your period, or first started taking birth control pills, you noticed your body is sensitive to hormonal events. Authors and hormone experts Sichel and Driscoll tell us that it's likely many of us have experienced "tremors" before, in the form of minor or short-lived emotional crises.

One in ten women is diagnosed with postpartum depression or anxiety, but experts suspect far more are affected. I've come across dozens of new moms barely holding their heads above water, and dozens more who told me they have had suicidal thoughts. So ill-informed are we, none of these women suspected their symptoms fit the profile of someone in postpartum distress.

I didn't report my first signs of distress, either, the day I remained prone on the couch, too tired to chase Patrick the Wonder Cruiser anymore. I had been angry at him all morning for keeping me up the night before, for refusing to be soothed, and milking me of all my energy, literally and figuratively.

Truthfully I had been snappish with him for quite a few mornings, and had taken to muttering "I hate my life" frequently under my breath. Duke was in the throes of a major career change, leaving the navy, which was his home as well as his job. He was being torn apart by this decision—at the same time I most needed his support and attention. But my impatience with Duke and his fears of what lay ahead for us, were not helping.

Most of all, I was mad at myself for not loving Patrick more. If

I truly loved him, I would enjoy being alone with him more. My long-awaited blessing, this beautiful child, had quickly become a dreaded burden. I tried to quiet my nagging feeling that I should never have become a mother.

The other mornings, Patrick had done something cute that snapped me out of my funk. Only this particular morning, his cuteness wasn't cutting it. I'd managed to nod off while he was in the Neglect-o-Matic, the name Duke and I had assigned to the automatic swing. Yet, the time the swing would satisfy him was growing shorter, so that Patrick was now liberated, padding along the bookshelves, and pillaging the books.

I saw him go for the heavy bookend, and had plenty of time to prevent the mishap. But I sat there and watched the bookend hurtle down on his foot, cutting him. This cut became Patrick's first scar—a quarter-inch, raised mark on the soft, flawless palette of his big toe. I knew I would see that scar every day for years to come—in bubble baths, swimming pools, and sandals.

I felt my selfishness had cut him, my inability to overcome mood swings I had conquered my entire life. I swallowed my shame, bandaged his foot, and made mental notes to be a better mommy from then on. Washing sippy cups in the sink and gazing out the window, I had to stop those little fantasies —the one where mommy got in the car and drove away—far, far away.

Dreams of Driving Away

Little did I know that so many other new moms were entertaining dreams of driving away. Most of us simply *fantasize* about disappearing on a cross-country drive. We have no intention of following through. Emma, a New York mother of two told me, "I imagine myself in a Jeep, heading toward somewhere quiet like the mountains or the ocean, to enjoy life as a single woman again." Emma doesn't want to dance on tables or stay out all night, though. "The crazy things I dream about include reading the newspaper uninterrupted and sipping coffee on a peaceful morning."

Longtime entertainer, now a radio show host, Marie Osmond was in the throes of undiagnosed postpartum depression when she took a long drive up the California coast, believing her seven children, including a newborn son, would be better off without her.

Fortunately, when Marie made her escape from a world that seemed to be closing in on her, she brought her cell phone. So, within a day, her husband came and rescued her, Marie put her suicidal thoughts to rest and went on to find healing medication and therapy. Also in her book, *Behind the Smile: My Journey Out of Postpartum Depression,* Marie describes camping out in a friend's extra bedroom and being nursed back to health. She exalts women and the way we huddle together in times of need. Only, she suggests, those of us in need have to reach out.

Survival Strategies for Moms on the Verge

Only problem is, new moms are so caught up in being perfect mothers that we're too ashamed to admit we need help. We stuff our feelings back into our spittle-stained sweatshirts and decide to apply ourselves even more heartily to the mission of mothering—despite how powerless, isolated, and afraid we feel.

Under this kind of stress, I believe moms on the verge have a couple of choices. We get to choose the kind of mental patient we want to resemble: the congenial jester in the sanitarium, or the recluse snarling at herself.

In the middle of the night, there isn't much choice. When your baby is colicky or teething, the night stretches out the way the rugged land must have for pioneer women taking families west by wagon train. Sometimes your spouse can intervene, but often babies only want comfort from the human that smells like milk. At 3 A.M., you become the recluse, snarling at the injustice of the situation and at your haunting deficiencies.

Come sunlight, it's easier to employ the following survival strategies my mommy compatriots and I endorse:

Wait Out the Stage

When you find yourself petting your car keys, visualizing a spontaneous and unending spa vacation, hold fast. There are things you can do to brighten the baby period.

Play to Your Strengths

Play to your strengths, even if the baby stage doesn't. Because I'm outgoing, excursions to Nordstrom's and its luxurious mother's lounge were my sanity amid Patrick's colic and my homebound loneliness. The lounge was an ideal "pick-up spot" for meeting empathetic, urban mommies. They made me feel considerably less freakish, since they, too, were only tolerating this legendary time with their newborns.

My sister, Catherine, who's always been a "nester" derived her comfort in the baby stage from a controllable routine inside her Kansas City home. She despised that it took longer to get Taylor out the door and strapped into his car seat than it would to complete the outing she'd planned. Catherine had lengthy and frequent personal-time breaks, because Taylor settled easily into his crib and loved to sleep. She beat the isolation, speaking to her best friend by phone nearly every day.

Play up Your Baby's Appeal

Secondly, optimize your tot's seductive appeal. Dress the baby to the nines. Put his bald head into goofy hats, and press ribbons and bows onto hers. Once I became a mom, my mother, Joyce, whispered to me the following sage advice: "When I liked what you girls were wearing, I found it easier to tolerate you."

Tolerate moi?! I know that's not the story of maternal adoration most of us prefer, especially from our own mothers. But it's honest and it works. The little oppressor is far less off-putting when dressed in a seersucker sailor suit.

Little Treats, Big Treats

Janine, whose irritable newborn was allergic to milk, derived comfort from hiring a contractor and revamping the home that at times seemed to imprison her. One New Jersey mom found the sight of neat closets as near to orgasmic as a postpartum woman can muster. She liked little spaces she could tackle and organize in the small breaks she had from child care.

One Boston mom, Susie, loved photographing her infant in funny, neck-supportive places all over the house and neighborhood. She figured her son was better off screaming and grimacing in artistic settings than perpetually in her overtired and restless arms.

The most important thing to remember, though, is that there's no sin in waiting out a stage. Lots of dads are uncomfortable with babies and to a certain extent, toddlers. "Who knows what to do with these little creatures," one father told me, "since they can't catch a ball, laugh at a joke, or help fix something outside?" In many cases, dads do not fully engage till later when their he-man skills fit their children's developmental stage.

Indeed, you can love a child and tend to him well without the orchestra playing. That's what we do in marriage, isn't it? We wait out an ambivalent period. A few months down the road, we re-learn that we are capable of renewed love, empathy, and tenderness. Even if it doesn't occur right off the bat, your son's or daughter's subsequent stages will likely bring out the best in you, the admirable qualities you envisioned having for *all* of parenthood.

Be Wary of "Wonder Babies"

Actress and postpartum depression survivor Brooke Shields recalls that in her infant's early months, she overheard her husband say that the baby was sleeping through the night. Rankled, Brooke retorted, "Whose household are *you* living in?!"

New moms, you see, look at nighttime feedings and sleep patterns through an entirely different prism than dads, or others, do. We keep track of exactly how much sleep we're missing, and tally the number of times our spouses snooze through a baby's fretting—even with the intercom set on the loudest volume.

Together with breast-feeding and child care, sleep is one of the "Big Three" subjects that cause new parents the most consternation because they inevitably attract comparisons. Fast-talkers don't realize how desperate new parents are for clues to a treasured night's sleep or a saner routine. Nor do they appreciate how loaded these topics are with implications about our aptness at parenthood or the personality of our little darling.

Remember there are no agreed-upon definitions in baby bragging. You'd think that seven to eight hours of zzzzz's would be the "through-the-night" standard. Yet, if you've heard the newborn two doors down is "sleeping through the night," this could mean she once conked out for the entire span of darkness, or that she regularly slumbers between midnight and five.

Know that babies who sleep longer may also be formula-fed, since formula makes infants feel fuller. But these distinctions are usually not shared. Similarly, you'll find that some parents do not consider part-time babysitters, or relatives who regularly oversee kids, a form of child care.

In truth, these details are no one's business. But if you are clawing for your place on the morality spectrum of motherhood and worry that you're the world's worst mother, details make a world of difference. That is why I was so gleeful to discover recently that an author who intimidated me with her proclaimed love of staying home full-time with children actually had a nanny the entire first decade of motherhood. I needed to know that we were, fundamentally, the same.

Fibs Over Feeding

Moms who breast-feed often feel compelled to fib. While the American Pediatric Association recommends breast-feeding for a year, cultural norms are so disparate that moms rarely know how their nursing testimonial will be received. We bend the truth to escape being accused of suckling sins, pro or con.

Only *you* know that medication, or a breast implant, prohibits you from breast-feeding. Maybe you never could get Samantha to latch, or you couldn't keep up with breast-feeding your Irish twins. All this information is too private to share with strangers.

Yes, breast is best. But it is also extraordinarily difficult. Moms today can rarely turn themselves over to one task—that of breast-feeding and getting enough rest to produce milk for a growing baby. I take solace in this big lie: Our secret embrace of what's right for us carries us through so many out-of-whack expectations.

Sift 'Til You Find Moms You Can Tolerate

Another important tactic in managing the "Big Three" and other maternal contests? Happy parents learn not to compare, but to *sift*. Meet and greet a lot of new moms, listen to their tales, and be vigilant about separating the wheat from the chaff.

Shalini, a Miami mother of three, including a set of twins, shared with me, "The mommies at my older daughter's ballet class made me want to go outside and smoke, the same way I felt in high school. They were so perfectly dressed and talked about such shallow things that I began to dread taking my daughter to her class."

Once Shalini got through the stressful patch of twin babyhood, she could work harder at finding moms with whom she could relate. Nevertheless, it's no picnic feeling that other moms are on top of the game, and that our shortcomings in the baby stage mean that we may be ill-suited to the *entire* parenting experience.

One suburban mom believes she'll never find iconoclastic mom friends, since none show up at their kids' preschool in biker jackets and nose rings like she does. But somewhere out there, I assure her, is a community of sympathetic—and body-pierced—moms and dads. It is worth sifting through parents and observing children, looking for those who more closely match you and yours.

Or, look for households to which you can pragmatically aspire. Quickly dispense of the playground advice or playgroup comparisons that inspire shame or despair. Hold up to yourself the suggestions and ideas that enhance your coloring, and the hues of your family life.

Lighten Up

Kind husbands are especially good at slaying the looming monsters our hormones and passions create. Brooke Shields remembers shedding tears in grocery stores, distraught over the soaring hope/dashed hope cadence of in vitro fertilization treatments. Self-conscious, she'd point out to TV producer husband Chris Henche, "I'm crying in the vegetable aisle." To which Henche quipped, "Would you like me to take you to the meat section?"

If you are husband-free like my friend Amelia, other tactics are equally good. Amelia adopted Laurel, a baby girl from Romania, who was walking by the time the papers were finalized, and Amelia brought her home to Nebraska. Laurel bonded to Amelia immediately, and wanted to be with her new mama every minute of the day. While Amelia had armfuls and lapfuls of love to offer, this "immediate and constant closeness" was also a shock to [her] system. Three months into motherhood, Amelia "lost it" in the bathroom and kept crying, "I can't do this." She remembers, "I felt as though my life had been taken away from me."

One problem was especially vexing: Amelia was constipated. Privacy in the bathroom to do her business proved impossible with a toddler demanding to be near. So Amelia called upon her mother and a support group of single adoptive moms she started herself— to regain her equilibrium. From the group, Amelia learned that other mothers left their screaming toddlers *outside* the door to go to the bathroom. And that an early bedtime for Laurel would give Amelia two solid hours of "alone time" every night.

In the forest of "I can't let my baby down or she'll be scarred for life," clarity of thought is hard to come by. You expect to place your young child's needs before your own, but you don't expect those needs to be so unceasing that your basic rights are trampled.

So you have to lighten up. Invite yourself and the baby over on a friend's laundry day, just to experience the semi-cogent world of other people's homes.

Eye Candy for Postpartum Moms

Devise an eye-candy plan. Eye-candy in this context isn't a muscle-clad construction worker taking a timely diet Coke break. It includes candles at Pier One, ducks at a lake, or the soup of the day at a local deli. It's a wash of beauty for tired eyes, a tiny thrill to get you through the days when your baby is frequently a pain in the rear. (Yes, it's really okay to say this . . . *it does not mean you don't love your baby!*)

Lightening up means you find funnier or rosier prisms with which to see early motherhood. Journaling or scrapbooking can sometimes divulge to us the sweetness, rather than the heaviness, of the tasks at hand. A glass of wine in the evening—in which even breast-feeding moms can indulge without harm to their babies—lends life a more relaxed tone. Duke's cousin, a mother of four, snuck in reading time during her shower, holding a paperback away from the spray.

Let Help In!

Recognize, too, that the more we push others away, insisting we can mother alone, the more susceptible we are to burnout and breakdowns. The more we allow our husbands to dismiss themselves from baby care, the longer we delay their being able to handle it. The more we insist on doing alone, the more that gets permanently assigned to us.

In retrospect, several moms told me they wished they had trusted babysitters with their infants earlier. But fear of babysitters, especially with small children, has become pervasive. New parents increasingly are reluctant to leave infants and toddlers with anyone but a relative, the nearly-impossible-to-find older lady, or a nanny from an exorbitant professional service.

My friends and I have bucked this trend, and I encourage you to do so, too—with high school or college-age sitters you trust, and with cell phone in hand. Duke and I left baby Patrick when he was six weeks old for ninety minutes with a teenager we'd spent time orienting and observing, who was babysitter certified, and who came recommended to us by friends. We also occasionally took sitters to malls with us so we could have dinner or shop while our blue-eyed wonder cruised in his stroller with his cute older girlfriend.

If you can't yet face an evening out, hand off your beloved daughter to the neighbor down the street who offered you a break. Feel proud that your baby is being exposed to a random act of kindness. Let yourself and her be enfolded into a community—the connectedness and support of which feminine values taught you to value.

Curl up for a nap, in silken eyeshades straight out of a vintage Hollywood movie, and laugh at the way you must look: unshaven, unclean but vaguely glamorous. See this postpartum party the way a jester would: a blur of frenetic motion and color brought on by a sodden mind and an even clumsier body. Then slumber, if only for an hour or two, before the next blurry party begins.

chapter four

I Love My Child, But I Loathe Motherhood

Making the Mommy Life More Fun

> **SECRET:** *Motherhood today is mission impossible. Learn to love your real self the way your kids do. Then get in a huddle.*

❀ "I really love being a dad," Duke sighed over the phone from his office, a few months into parenthood. This should have been a tender moment, a turning point in which a big, scruffy man confessed his enchantment with a toothless smidge of a boy. Duke's proclamation could have deepened our marriage, and reminded me of the pureness of affection that had propelled us down the aisle three years before.

Instead, I cackled at him, "*Of course* you love being a dad! You're at work all day and when you come home, you play with the baby for an hour before he goes to bed! Who *wouldn't* love being a dad?!"

In home videos Duke recorded at the time, I play developmental games with Patrick, and kiss the baby with hilarious frequency. It's clear I love and cherish my little son. Nevertheless, the hostility I felt toward my role as Mama was thinly veiled. Several years passed before I could articulate and admit: I adore my children but much of the time, I despise being a mother.

It's likely many of you think it's not possible for this dichotomy to exist in a sane, healthy person, particularly someone in charge of raising two children and a childlike husband. But I've come to believe embracing this paradox keeps modern mothers sane.

Why do I, and many women less apt to confess it, sometimes abhor being mothers? Mostly because we can't meet the exhaustive standards required of "a good mother," according to today's definition. Shari Thurer, Ph.D., a Boston University professor and psychologist, says that over the last forty years, culture has added each maternal ideal to the last, rather than replace one with another. In many ways, the enormous role we are required to play has made motherhood a lose-lose proposition.

Eileen, a mother of two in Iowa, describes her frustration with modern expectations, saying, "I'm responsible for how my son turns out. Yet, I'm also limited in the discipline I can use. In other words, society doesn't trust me to spank my kid responsibly, but I'm the one society blames if my son gets out of line."

A mother of three in Boston who quit her job as an attorney to stay home with her children concludes, "Motherhood is by far the hardest job I've ever done. But I've never figured out how to make it *sound* impressive."

In this chapter, we'll take a look at how motherhood became the depository for so many wacky and contradictory ideals. Moms today tackle considerable disadvantages as compared to previous generations, which we'll demonstrate. Then win-win moms will tell you how they made motherhood more fun and less taxing.

Your Mom and You

My mom tells my sister and me, "Motherhood never felt like a sacrifice to me because I loved you so much." I don't question my mom's big-heartedness but moms of her generation also expected to deny themselves. They anticipated sacrificing work for full-time child care, with plans to eventually return to paid employment.

Men and women today are not conditioned for the degree of sacrifice that parenthood, and above all motherhood, requires. This is, I believe, the reason the transition to parenthood is so volatile for us, and why so many of us have a personality conflict with the baby stage.

Most of us develop more respect and empathy for our mothers and the sacrifices they made for us after we join the ranks of motherhood ourselves. Nevertheless, approximately 82 percent of us believe we are doing as good a job, or a better job with our children than our mothers did with us, according to *Parenting* magazine.

Any way you look at it, parenthood is much harder today than when we were small. Despite having options —to work at home or outside the home, to have babies or not—we *feel* we have few real choices. The new world that was supposed to accommodate smart, career-oriented moms and equal partnerships in marriage never materialized en masse.

Postpartum Support Meant Neighbors and Casseroles

Neighbors, coffee klatches, and church call-chains rallied around new parents of my mother's generation, making possible time off from Baby and iceboxes stocked with casseroles. Although we have mandated maternity and paternity leaves, support today is not comparable to that which many of our moms received, when a great number of women were still at home and readily chipped in to help one another's families.

Stay-at-Home Was the Norm

While many women in our mothers' middle- and upper-middle-class circles received college degrees and spent some time in professional life, most also relinquished work when they had children. Though their material expectations were modest, our moms could, in many instances, afford to stay home with us full-time when we were small.

Today 65 percent of moms with small children are in the workplace. According to *Time* magazine, economic conditions demand that 60 percent of us are in the workplace to pay for bills, not to garner extravagances. Some of us work outside the home because we would otherwise be unfulfilled and thus intolerable mommies. But the mommy majority prefers part-time or flexible hours, which are hard to come by in our seemingly evolved marketplace.

Dads Stuck Around

Decades ago, having children solidified marriage, according to the statistics. These days couples who take the parenthood plunge increase their chances of divorce.

Our fathers and their fathers were the primary, if not only, breadwinners in our families, and were not expected to devote much time to child care. Today, husbands and fathers fully expect to be engaged in child care and have taken up a bigger role. In fact, as leisure time in America shrinks, many dads today feel gypped, unable to devote the hours to their children that they intended to.

There used to be an enormous stigma attached to being a single mother. Today single motherhood is accepted, even admired, and a much larger percentage of families are run by single-mom heads of households.

Our Parents Were Younger, Both in Years and Experiences

As youngsters, we ran circles around our moms the same way our children dizzy us. But most of our moms were in their twenties and enjoyed the staple of energy that younger adults possess.

Today, men and women are waiting longer to marry and have children, making us five to fifteen years older—and considerably more fatigued—than previous generations of parents. Virtually unheard of in our moms' day, some modern women are experiencing first-time motherhood in their forties and fifties.

Experts tell us that older parents do make better parents, lending greater stability, confidence and patience to this most exacting of jobs. Yet, greater complications beset over-thirty parents.

Moms of our era face a previously unimaginable double whammy: the tribulations of early motherhood simultaneous to the onset of menopause. The single mother of a four-year old she adopted from China, Cathy in Phoenix is coping the best she can. "Menopause, including the surgery I had last fall to ease some symptoms, has been difficult. I make every effort not to inflict my grumpiness on my daughter but I am sure sometimes she senses it."

As older moms, we are more apt to feel the pinch of being in the sandwich generation and the need to care for aging parents as well. "My parents are in terrible health," Keesha from Detroit says. "I can't tell you how much pressure I'm under, working full-time, trying to take care of two kids under the age of five, getting them to the doctor at the same time I'm taking my father to the doctor, or going with my mom to buy a new walker."

We're older in years and in experiences. Those of us who enjoyed independent, career-focused, and self-indulgent but also self-defining years, feel every ounce of sacrifice involved in mothering. Brought up to seek self-fulfillment and individual happiness, we are not wired the same way as was the so-called "greatest generation" who lived during World War II. We were not immersed from birth in societal values that prized God and country, much less duty.

Indeed, researchers at San Diego State University report that older, wealthier couples grapple most with the transition to parenthood. In their formula for happiness, the salaried thirty- and forty-something set includes dinners out, frequent travel, and having time for themselves and their romantic lives. So their sense of deprivation and of having lost their modus operandi is often intense.

Intensive Mothering

Dr. Benjamin Spock encouraged our moms to trust their instincts. But we are subjected to the criteria of "intensive mothering," so named by University of Virginia professor Sharon Hays in *The Cultural Contradictions of Motherhood*. Intensive mothering is demanding, child-centered, expert-guided, labor-intensive, and expensive, Hays says. Ironically, these demands come at a time when 75 percent of all American mothers are in the labor force, nearly 40 percent of them in full-time jobs.

Women accustomed to being overachievers embraced these outrageously heightened ideals for mothering. So that today, many of us manically second-guess ourselves, trying to do everything by the book, or by twenty child-care books that contradict each other. We throw galalike birthday parties for our kids and teach them to overdo and overspend, rather than appreciate simpler and less fabricated delights.

Zen and the Art of Macaroni Maintenance

Making this corpulent job even more ungainly has been the recent romanticization of motherhood. With the exception of Roseanne Barr and a few others in the last decade or two, the media has portrayed mommyhood as the ultimate form of fulfillment, a diaper-changing form of Zen.

In her 2000 book *Flux: Women on Sex, Work, Love, Kids, and Life in a Half-Changed World,* Peggy Orenstein reports that starting in the 1990s, "motherhood supplanted marriage as the source of romantic daydreams" for childless, unmarried women in their twenties and early- to mid-thirties. Far more so than marriage, Orenstein learned, "motherhood has become increasingly central to women's conception of femininity."

Aimee, an Orange County, California, mother of three, says she's had it up to here with moms who pretend everything in their world is wonderful. "The way I see it, I'm a mom and for that reason, I need ten good reasons every day not to go postal. That's the unromantic truth about motherhood."

Marketing to Moms

In large part, the media's touting of seamless motherhood has been fueled by advertisers who increasingly recognize the consumer-power mothers wield. An explosion of media vehicles—new magazines, catalogs, cable stations, TV shows, and films—has enabled corporations to bombard us with messages about must-have products to achieve perfect parenting.

The popular media also preys on a mother's deepest fears, exaggerating the risk of child abduction and featuring stories such as "Is your home toxic?" and heartbreaking tales of children with rare diseases. It's no wonder then, that moms feel they must be on constant alert. Researchers tell us dads experience their deepest relaxation in the presence of their families, while moms always feel they are on duty with their families and only relax when away from them.

According to *Remedy* magazine, homemakers who take vacations once every six years or less are twice as likely to have a heart attack as those who take vacations two or more times a year. As it turns out, maxed-out moms may be the biggest hazards in our homes, the ones truly in need of caring precautions and child-proofing.

A navy friend of ours, whose pilot husband was deployed and away for six months, put her baby intercom out front of her home and jogged around the block during her two- and four-year-old boys' naps. Never mind that the Swedes routinely leave babies sleeping in bassinets when they go grocery shopping. Our jogger friend was chastised by the mommies at the playground who suggested every possible risk, none of them bigger to my way of thinking than that of a mommy losing her mind—taking care of two boys 24/7 all by herself for six long months on a military salary that wouldn't cover child-care help.

Making Motherhood More Fun

Here, though, we're dropping the façade. No more pretending that we're all-sacrificing moms who would never dream of leaving our children's sides to exercise. Those of us who grew up idolizing the

Bionic Woman have to make it okay for all of us to be human and to have needs. This is the first step to making motherhood more manageable and certainly more fun.

Say "Uncle"

If the expectations of modern motherhood have you in a choke-hold, it's time you said "Uncle." Stop fighting. Give up.

I know how hard this is for you alpha females, household divas, efficiency mavens, and germ-a-phobes. But you must let go of delusions you foster about being a mommy with perfect hair or a tidy playroom.

Those of you who have "a way with children" think you're immune, too. Yet, Christine from Vermont shares, "I had taken care of people's children for years but it is so different to be *completely* responsible for a human being. I was also accustomed to working ten-hour days. But now I'm on-duty *all* the time. There's no comparison." Even women who live in shoes and want gaggles of children around them are surrendering.

Still think you are going to overcome all the hurdles and be crowned Mom Extraordinaire? This is my final shot at persuading you: Christine shares parenting responsibilities with her lesbian partner. And she says that even with *two* moms working at it, the job of caring for a little one is still overwhelming. "My partner is my soul mate, and it's wonderful to raise a child with someone who shares the burden of nurturing. Nevertheless we're far more exhausted and haggard than we expected to be."

Indeed, we cannot mother according to *other* people's rules. Who could, given that our society needs mothers in the economy but doesn't address child-care concerns? That believes welfare moms should work and well-to-do moms should stay home? That insists children benefit from more time with parents but demands mom and dad work more hours? That demands schools have "zero tolerance" for kindergarteners tussling on a playground, but salivates over guns and violence?

Even without nonsensical cultural expectations, kids are brutal. In our pre-parenting days, most of us believe that the out-of-control nature of life with munchkins would be offset by the joy they bring. Unfortunately the balance sheet in the early years turns out not to be so tidy.

Annie, a New Jersey stay-at-home mom said it well: "I imagined the mother-child relationship being reciprocal. I expected to be filled up by the love my children expressed, and by my enormous pride in them. Little did I know that I'd be skimming a layer of cream off the top. The fulfillment is thick and sweet, but often there's not a lot of it."

Parenting the Private Way

You must stop turning to others—either to society or to your children—for the gratitude you need to mother on. Instead, parent the private way. Write your own code. Stop looking for public approval and start thrusting your staff out in front of you, waiting for big seas of Cheerios to part.

Author Jane Smiley, mother of three, shared her secret in *The New York Times Magazine* a few years ago. "After all these years, I have decided that the only true state of motherhood is the private one." Smiley goes on to describe a time she volunteered in her son A. J.'s kindergarten class. She says A. J. managed to contain his glee at having Mom there through the Pledge of Allegiance, the three-cornered hat song, and the sign-language lesson starting with N. "But then my presence was simply too much for him and he rose from his carpet square and began kissing me all over until I took him into my lap and held him tightly."

Smiley continues:

It is not that such moments make motherhood worth it; it is that they *are* motherhood—a woman's subjective experience of being a mother. Every mother has them, day after day. If I had learned to focus on them 20 years ago rather than pay attention to the opinions of others, I would probably have fewer regrets.

Slay the beast of expectations. Stop believing that experts have methods that will work for you. Understand that the intimate dance begun at birth in which your child expresses need and you respond is the only choreography you need to know. Maternal intuition does exist, only we have to be quiet enough to sense it and confident enough in ourselves to let it lead us.

Relearn to Be You

When you were little, it was fun to pretend to be a superhero. Now that you're grown up, you need to be able to tell the difference between real and pretend.

Admit your human-ness first painfully to yourself, and then to those keeping score on the outside. Similar to the first time you asked for an extension on a paper in college, being granted human status can feel as bad as it does good.

Divorced and single moms know these emotions well. They absorb the pain of discovering there are limits to a love that was supposed to last forever, as well as limits inherent in being a single mom. With divorce, my college friend in Minnesota taught me,

"You do start flying under the radar of social pretenses, in both good and bad ways. You lose the more admirable status of the traditional family. Then again, single mothers don't feel guilty about working because they are the family's central or sole financial providers."

Yet, stripping yourself of veneers can be very freeing. Believe it or not, you will eventually really like the person you discover you are—the woman no longer able to relish having a tiny waist, Cat-woman sex appeal, an on-track career, a chicly furnished home, and a happily-ever-after marriage. The "real you" will take some getting used to, as she likely went underground at about age nine. But soon, I promise, you'll grow to love the integrity and realness she represents.

Kids Love the Real You

More likely though, you will start seeing yourself through the eyes of your children. A fellow navy wife, Sharon, in Florida, began to cry when she told me, "My kids have seen me at my best and my very worst. And in the end, day after day of seeing plain old me, they love me. They love me for me."

Two sentences later, Sharon bemoans her postnatal figure. But for one freeze-frame, Sharon let herself be loved, instead of believing that affection and favor should be withheld from her until she becomes the woman she is always berating herself to be.

I am always struck by the way my son Patrick looks at me. It's the way I yearned for men to look at me, from about age nine on. Every night now, my dance card is full, because I have two adoring partners, Patrick and his brother, Liam. I don't wonder if they'll call, I'm not subject to endless disappointments . . . not yet, anyway. My boys are stalwart admirers, even though they've perpetually seen me in my least composed, least confident, least attractive stage of life.

In this respect, marriage is bound to be dethroned by little ones.

Even if you experienced unconditional love for the first glorious time with your mate, a child's love is a whole other level of unconditional. You simply cannot believe that someone would burst from a school bus, arms outstretched and singing your name: "Mommy, Mommy!" Nor is there anything on this earth that compares with the feeling that you are the balm a little person carries with him through an entire day in the big, scary world that exists apart from you.

By accepting yourself as a limited but loved human being, you tap into an adrenaline stream of parenthood. You're able to be more playful in the midst of ridiculous stress, and to derive pleasure from being a member of this club of fools.

Commit to Radical Pruning

Once you've embraced "you, glorious you" the next step is to prune. At an heirloom roses seminar at a local nursery, I learned: To enable the plant to thrive and grow in the direction you want it to grow, you have to be brutal about dispensing with smaller branches heading elsewhere. Personally, I've had to whack off what felt to me like major chunks of my soul. But it turned out, I only lost pretense, I didn't lose my soul.

Duke and a horde of bachelor and stranded naval officers in Washington State will attest that while my four-month-old fussed upstairs in the arms of a babysitter, I served a Christmas goose for 16—with bone china, silver, and crystal—the works! Mind you, the goose took bloody forever—at least two rounds of running upstairs and breast-feeding—and everyone was sloshed by the time "my goose was cooked."

My love of gathering friends around a gracious table is very much alive. But I've temporarily at least become an aficionado of paper plates, barbecue grills, and child-friendly dinners. I've learned that elaborate preparations and playing hostess were often my ways of avoiding having to really open up and talk to people. Not to mention that by placing a higher value on entertaining sixteen than entertaining one tiny boy, I wasn't letting baby love in.

Motherhood ultimately calls us to *be* and not do. Granted this is very threatening: admitting defeat, accepting yourself, and then paring down. But just as in rose gardens, these tips will give your most fundamental strengths a chance to grow.

Let your *Travel & Leisure* subscription expire. Go to work with undone nails. Let the little darling take an occasional Lunchable to school, or watch a six-hour span of TV one Saturday while you sleep. Bark at the relatives who insist you host Easter dinner. In other words, find ways you can cut back on being sensational so that you have a little humor, patience, and kindness left for those you truly cherish.

Do you have a choice? Yes. You can keep doing everything, and the rage you feel at the unmanageability of it all will turn a loving comment into a sarcastic snarl. Your anger at the betrayal of everything your mom and a host of progressive thinkers promised you would have, will eat away at your marriage, and eventually at the relationship you have with your son or daughter. There's plenty more talk to come of the rage that mamas feel, and how to cope with it. But for now, take only baby steps: Cut back before the tension chokes off all the affection and gladness you feel.

Huddle

Not since powder-puff football at Southwest High School in Kansas City have I appreciated the role of the "huddle." You get shoulder to shoulder with some other sweaty, unkempt women;

muscle your way into some semblance of a team; and you figure out how to get the small ball down the big field together.

When you read Anita Diamant's *The Red Tent*, you get the same feeling of community. Only she writes of ancient times, in which women congregated in a separate tent during menstruation, late pregnancy, delivery, and for months postpartum. An experienced midwife and the tribe's mothers and daughters understood from watching and caring for each other, the cycles of life and the passions and demons each stage can inspire. Inevitably then, they recognized fault lines and tremors, and knew what to do for a mother whose happy disposition suddenly soured.

There's no question it takes a village—a way of life still practiced by many cultures today. But what do we do in the absence of a sisterhood that can nourish, massage, listen, and reassure us when we're melting down or breaking down? Namely, you borrow a page from our mothers' history book and you reach out.

I make and deliver a hot dinner to new moms in my neighborhood, church, or preschool—even those I haven't yet met. A roasted chicken and a bottle of wine is my way of signaling to moms that we belong to a community and that we can call on each other.

The "mommy tell-all" nights I hosted while researching this book were the catalyst behind moms' groups that formed in San Diego. I call these groups "mompools" because like carpools, they are strategic exchanges that preserve our energy and allow us to share the burdens of motherhood. My mompool meets twice a month, and consists of seven to ten moms who gather at each others' homes after their kids are asleep to build community, vent, and problem-solve. (For more on how to start your own mompool, see page 244).

Another popular huddling option is the Friday-night neighborhood cocktail hour, in which moms trade off hosting wine and cheese. While kids play in the backyard or house, these harried gals convene to trade complaints, secrets, and sisterhood.

My favorite, though, is a healthy cooking club in which women pay a personal chef to gather and prep enough ingredients for a week's worth of nutritional dinners. Then, together on a Sunday night at a local church or community center with a professional kitchen, they prepare and cook the family cuisine each of them will take home for the week. Of course, the conversations they enjoy together are as good for them as the low-fat food their families consume all week.

There are, in many cities now, alliances and support groups for postpartum women who are struggling. There, you can meet or be referred to doctors and therapists who specialize in postpartum health with whom you can also huddle.

It's good for fathers, too, to see how other families function, how other dads struggle, and to find men who also forego golf or surfing to spend time with their small children. Mingling their machismo, they will feel less threatened and may be more willing to take the next steps: spot you more with the kids, cut back at work, volunteer at a child's school, attend religious services with the family, or take a parenting class.

Being in a huddle, you'll delight in motherhood again. You'll like the title *mother*. In the context of a community that lets us rest, shares our burdens, and takes responsibility for children, too, motherhood can be life's most privileged and fulfilling role.

The Wacky Things Moms Do

In the slap-happy world of diapers and the damned, moms find themselves doing outrageous things to satisfy their kids or preserve their good-mommy façade. Here are some examples from my ensemble:

"To help my kids build their collections, I called all the McDonald'ses and Burger Kings in our area to find out which toy they were distributing with kids' meals."

"As much a pacifist as I am, I've resorted to cutting my boys' food into the shape of guns to get them to eat them."

"I once drove 75 miles out of town so my daughter, who fell asleep in the car, got her full, uninterrupted nap."

"My son's school prohibited parents from campus during the day. Although administrators assured me they had handled the problem, I hid in the bushes with binoculars for three days during recess to make sure my son was not getting bullied."

"I took the baby to see a doctor in the clinic. When he didn't prescribe antibiotics, I left his office, went out to the lobby, and registered again. The next doctor gave us the prescription we needed."

"My daughter is obsessed with a certain shade of pink. All her clothes and shoes have to be the same hue, or she won't put them on. For a year, she only ate pink food."

Mother's Acts of Self-Preservation

Parents are likewise pushed to extremes when they need rest or a few minutes of calm. I'm not endorsing their methods, but here are samples of their madness:

"Occasionally I resort to Benadryl. A dose at bedtime ensures a far better night's sleep for all of us."

"We had no money for babysitters so we took our kids to Sunday school at a local church. Then my husband and I stole away to have breakfast together."

"I needed a break so badly that I told my husband that my business trip was two days longer than it really was. I spent two days ordering room service and watching mindless cable."

"I turned the stereo up full blast in my car and screamed at the top of my lungs."

"In large part, I picked my son's preschool because the hours permitted me to get to my 9:30 aerobics class." ❧

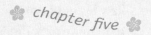

chapter five

To Work or Not to Work?

Finding the Choice That's Right for You

> **SECRET:** *The work/life balance is elusive—for all moms. Choose the right mix for you and your family, and reevaluate frequently.*

For three brief months prior to Patrick's first birthday, I had it all. Anticipating the launch of my book *What No One Tells the Bride,* I'd come up with an ingenious plan: I hired an aspiring writer and college student to live with us for the summer and perform child care in exchange for the experience she'd receive: helping a writer promote and sell her book. With her help, I could bring Patrick with me to book signings, readings, and appearances, since Duke was deployed on an aircraft carrier in the Persian Gulf.

That summer, I had the most fun I've ever had, mingling two loves of my life—my son and my writing. In-home help also enabled me to gear up for bigger breadwinning—much needed because while we were expecting, Duke had learned that cutbacks in the navy were now so severe as to prevent his career climb. So, at thirty-five, Duke decided to start over, exploring opportunities in the civilian world. Over the summer, I finished a book proposal, the sale of which would be our sole income if Duke's job search was prolonged and our savings dwindled.

Those magical weeks flew by, until Amanda returned to school and Patrick and I packed up to move to Southern California, where Duke was already job-hunting. My bride book sales progressed slowly at first, while a subsequent book, *A New Mom's Bill of Rights,* was rejected by publishers.

Hiring freezes in dotcoms and telecommunications companies made Duke's employment elusive. We bickered constantly, as I offered job-hunting advice and he ignored every suggestion I made. Sweltering in a breezeless two-bedroom rental, I learned nannies in San Diego were unaffordable, as was most day care. For that matter, we were unsure how we'd pay the bills stacking up on the coffee table.

This was, by the way, the month I started taking Prozac. Just a smidge, the family doctor said, to take the edge off this stressful time. After all, I felt as if my writing career was over. My husband and I had nothing in common anymore. And as much as I had wanted children, I believed I was a terrible mother. As much fun as Patrick had become as a toddler, I could not imagine managing him at home full-time, which appeared to be the only financially viable option.

What About What *Mom* Wants?

A few months later, Duke signed a contract with a consulting firm, and we bought a three-bedroom home built in 1908—historic by California standards. We found ideal home day care for Patrick, with a provider who loved him as her own and whose values were strikingly similar to ours. We even decided to try to have another baby—the stresses of which we feared, but took on because we wanted Patrick to have a sibling.

I was writing regularly for a national magazine audience and gaining more lucrative clients in public relations and website work, but my salary never seemed to exceed our child-care costs. Increasingly Duke's career became the priority, his hours more extensive while my talent got back-burnered.

I believed in putting family first, only I could not understand why that always meant Mom, a full-fledged member of the family, had to come last. Sure, Duke was changing careers in his thirties, but why did his job have to dominate? He had not even *tried* to negotiate a flexible schedule when he was hired. He didn't spend every workday calculating the precise number of hours his son had been in day care, nor drop everything to rush to get Patrick, so that our sweet boy got ample time and attention from a loving parent.

Trying to compose singing phrases with Patrick there was useless. As a run-about, he cheated death and dismemberment so many times every day—bumps, scrapes, and bruises proliferating on his soft skin– that close supervision was barely enough. On weekends, when Duke tried to give me breaks, Patrick preferred me, and Duke did not know how to engage or distract Patrick in all the ways I had learned to do.

Increasingly, I saw that my husband did not have the patience or skills to care for Patrick for more than a two-hour stretch. I was anxiety-ridden any time I was out, and Duke was so exasperated when I returned that any pleasure I'd derived from writing time was quickly flattened.

Talking to other mothers, everyone said, "So you'll take a temporary break from writing." Or they proffered, "If you died tomorrow, wouldn't you be glad you spent your last remaining days with your toddler?" I felt like a heathen but I could not concede those points. How could I take a break in the competitive stream of a writing career, now that I'd finally achieved some success? The truths I sought at the keyboard were as much a part of me as my son. Having written obsessively since I was a little girl, I wasn't sure how to set it aside.

I couldn't deny Patrick what I knew he needed, I couldn't find any peace with the competing priorities, and I couldn't make our lives work the progressive way we had envisioned when we flung contraception to the stars and started our family. If I couldn't do it, with so many advantages in my corner, I knew other women with bigger burdens and complications had to be failing, too.

To Stay at Home or Return to Work?

Francine Deutsch, Ph.D., professor of psychology at Mount Holyoke College, found that 58 percent of at-home and 53 percent of mommies working outside the home reported feeling frustrated, depressed, hopeless, or angry. That's what I found, too, when I delved into work questions: women in both camps are full of angst about their situations.

Among others, Dr. Phil and Dr. Laura deride parental selfishness, saying, "You chose to have a baby so now deal with the consequences." Yet, they didn't see what I saw: Hurting mommies were already sucking it up, already putting their children's and families' needs first even if finances required that they work. Over the long term, though, the repercussions of the disappointments moms stuffed inside were corrosive. The "put up and shut up" approach does not take into account that family life centering round a toxic mommy cannot forever be spared lethal effects.

Stresses of Staying at Home

Scores of moms I know relinquish work to stay home with little ones but are dissatisfied or frustrated a good portion of the time. They are clumsy introducing themselves, half-mumbling what they used to do for work in a previous life, or resorting to a browbeaten "Just a mom." Shut inside with two children with chicken pox for a week, I understand how very desperate the situation is for them, how on-the-precipice they feel, even though their husbands don't often recognize it.

Sally, a mother of two in Indiana, imagined she'd be the perfect stay-at-home mom because she's very nurturing. "I now realize I need to get out and have more time alone than full-time mother-hood allows," Sally says. "More than that, there are times I don't en-joy being a mom. I never expected to have those feelings. I get so overwhelmed and frustrated, and I am not the person I want to be with them." Unable to accept her emerging Jekyll and Hyde per-sonalities at home, Sally returned to full-time work. Indeed, re-searchers tell us, work seems to buffer new moms from depression, and stay-at-home moms have harder emotional travails.

After all, guilt is an equal opportunity employer. Mommies at home feel guilty for not making the most of their college educa-tions and alternatively for not being able to master household tasks given their supposedly freer schedules. Frequently, moms at home expressed their frustration at feeling sluggish and stuck, unable to complete a multitude of projects with which they'd charged them-selves. "I could gaze at my daughter all day long," says a former lin-gerie designer with a six-month-old dumpling. "It's almost easier to succumb to doing one thing rather than fourteen. Except at the end of the day, I can't believe how little I've accomplished."

Stresses of Salaried Mommies

To my eyes anyway, women who worked full-time at relatively family-friendly companies seemed ever so slightly healthier. Their children were in day care and at least not presently exhibiting ax-murderer tendencies. These women retained some confidence, and a modicum of salary-fueled decision-making power in their households.

Of course these wonder-women were utterly stressed out and secretly ashamed to welcome the start of a workweek when they could leave their children in the care of others. They also missed some of parenthood's biggest rewards—first steps or first poops in potties, or school pageants in which kindergarteners wore bonnets and warbled songs about springtime. The two or three hours after work with their children were stomach-taut tense, as everyone was exhausted and grumpy, homework and baths beckoned, and dinner was thrown together. To top it off, a child's cold or fever inspired negotiations between spouses and Palm Pilots more complex than those that precede treaty signings.

Only in glossy magazines in the height of the dotcom boom can I find examples of parents successfully tag-teaming child care, through shift work or reduced schedules for both mom and dad. Only through friends of friends of friends do I hear about "sequencing" and moms who gracefully surrender work to raise children, only to return to career success years later.

I once read about an executive at IKEA who was encouraged to nurse her baby during an interview for a promotion, but know no one who has experienced anything remotely similar. I also read about stay-at-home dads, but I don't know a single one in my child-filled neighborhood. According to statistics, dads who take over the role of primary caregiver do so mostly as a stopgap or emergency measure. Studies show only 20 percent of dads serving as primary caregivers will still be *numero uno* parent two years later.

The Stresses All Moms Share

Here's the reality I experience firsthand: friends who bounce babies and checks, as couples try to maneuver a lost or reduced income and/or the heavy costs of diapers, child care, preschool, feeding, clothing, and entertaining their little kids. For reasons scientists don't understand, couples still base economic and "who will work and how much" decisions on the formula in which child-care costs are charged against Mom's salary only. While it's true that a woman's salary is still apt to be less than her husband's, there's no good reason for couples not to approach choices, considering child care a cost to be absorbed by their joint incomes.

Whether by choice, or because they had smaller salaries, lots of moms I know who quit full-time employment started innovative Internet-driven or home-based businesses such as selling Mary Kay cosmetics or Weekenders clothing, but none of them did so to pay the mortgage.

Alternately my friends who shine in their offices, law firms, and on sales staffs become masters of the faked calendar or the forwarded office phone, rarely able to be truly candid with their employers about their needs as mothers.

Many of us approached motherhood the same way we did marriage: to enhance, not complete our lives. We envisioned hoisting Baby in a backpack and going on with the lives we had already established. Little did we know that we would meet our match, when the real needs of babies and little ones exposed the limits of our energy, our marital partnerships, and our forward-thinking companies.

Does Daddy Help, Or Complicate, the Situation?

Missing from many of our baby-makes-threesomes are spouses who share family duties equally, and defend our careers as energetically as their own. The men we married became more involved parents than their dads were. But the pledge they made to be "involved"—even actively—turns out to be a far cry from "responsible for" or "in-charge" to the extent most moms become.

How startling it is to find that although your spouse shares basic parenting with you, he does not experience the anguish and indecision, the guilt and frustration that tears at many a mom's soul every day. He leaves for work in the above-it-all way he always does, unaware of how many diapers are left, where the kids have stashed their cleats, or when tuition is due. And because the father of your children cannot relate to the pain and injustice of this, your sarcasm and rage start blacking out all the good stuff he represents.

The golden rule of the equal rights movement, that nature can be overcome by nurture, becomes a piñata in early motherhood. The impact of a husband's laissez-faire parenting style sets it reeling. Choices that are often too poor to be considered true choices dull the swing of our hopes, forcing them into a prescribed back-and-forth route. But the biggest blow is often from our own physiology—mammary glands, cuddle hormones, hairs on the backs of our necks, and frogs in our tummies that tell us we are mothers, body and soul, and indeed deep down in our bones.

Many moms believe their husbands' lapses as fathers are due to DNA. Because even dads who jump with two feet into the muddy waters of parenting don't get preoccupied about being good fathers and don't experience the constant gnawing of details and concerns that mothers do. I would venture that moms spend as much time thinking about kids as men spend thinking about sex.

In *The Price of Motherhood: Why the Most Important Job in the World Is Still the Least Valued,* author Ann Crittenden sums it up well: "For all the change of the last decade, one thing has stayed the same: It is women who adjust their lives to accommodate children; who do what is necessary to make a home; who forego status, income, advancement and independence."

The Price Women Pay

According to Crittenden, women who pursue careers first and children later do achieve more, and gain higher salaries, than those who choose the opposite timing. Try marrying early in your career or having children at a younger age and you'll likely never catch up with your childless peers in income potential.

If you're a college-educated American woman and you quit or cut back on work after the kids arrive, you'll forego, on average, $1 million dollars in income. And your pension will be much smaller. Not to mention that child-care workers receive social security credits while stay-at-home moms don't.

Stay engaged in the workplace as a mom and you'll book hours longer than almost anyone else in the economy. Even if you are the bigger breadwinner, you'll log thirteen hours a week more on child-care and household chores than your co-parent. In families with preschool children, moms typically put in three to four times the hours that dads do.

And motherhood is the single biggest risk factor for poverty. We've already mentioned that divorce rates increase among couples with children. This does not bode well for moms in forty-seven of fifty states (California, New Mexico, and Louisiana being the exceptions) with no legal right to half the assets in a marriage, should it dissolve.

Blaming the Bra-Burners

Wahoo, isn't this the fabulous double-scoop life Gloria and her bra-burning gal pals wanted for us?! Not at all, though many moms blame either their husbands or our feminist foremothers for their distress. Sure, the idea was for us to do a man's job, but it was also for a man to feel the profound connection moms do to their children, and adjust their lives to fortify a family.

A few years ago, when Gloria Steinem became a first-time bride at sixty-something, she said on National Public Radio that for our generation, marriage is no longer the institution that stifles and diminishes us. Today, she said, motherhood is the ultimate obstacle for feminists. All of us continue to have to declare a loss in one major area of our lives—either a loss of financial and career stability, or a loss of time and attention we believe our children deserve.

To top it off, moms who go off to work—with the exception of welfare moms, of course—are chastised for "letting others raise them," or "refusing to downgrade your standard of living to be at home," or "ignoring the desire of small children to be with their parents."

Moms who raise children as their full-time job home are called "stay-at-home" when they are hardly ever at home, shuttling back and forth between schools, errands, and activities. They are also presumed to be lazy, indulgent, boring, cliché, and all in all, less sexy.

Find Your Own Way

If you can imagine it, most moms get used to entertaining this torment about work and family and settle into the ridiculous demands of primary parenthood. Within a few years, we stop thrashing about so much and learn to squeeze enjoyment from these circumstances. We may ache about long-term damage to our confidence, future aspirations, health, and financial stability. We even accept that we were shanghai-ed when it came to our careers and our dreams of equal parenting. The tradeoff is that we get far bigger portions of the deliciousness of children than our husbands receive.

Many of us befriend moms in our same at-home or at-work categories to avoid these judgments or associations. However, this book has a higher calling: We have to honor moms for making choices that are right for them and their families. Different choices threaten us deeply, and force us to engage in a painful internal dialogue. But if we make a rule that no raised eyebrows or "cluck, clucks" are allowed, maybe we have a chance at working together rather than being turned into mud wrestlers over issues that stun the hearts of *all* mothers.

In our experience, four steps help moms find their way:

Ask, "Is This a Good Fit for Me?"

When I was single and ruled by my career, I thought it was ludicrous for my peers not to know, before their maternity leaves, whether they would come back to work. "How could a respectable woman not know her own mind? Could a baby turn a woman into complete mush?" I thought.

These days, I admire ambivalence in expectant mothers. These women grasp the enormity of emotion a child brings, and give themselves permission to feel what they feel, even if it is vastly different than what they expected.

Ultimately, according to several mom executives, women cannot "plan" the right mix of work and family life because life's many twists and turns require even the best plans to change. Take it from the president of Medalia Communications and the former vice president and group publisher of Working Woman Network, Delia Passi Smalter, who by thirty, had three daughters, divorced, and then functioned as a single mother. She says women shouldn't feel pressured to follow a prescribed path. "I never planned to have children so early, but when it happened my family took precedence and my career went into neutral for six or seven years."

Having adopted two children, an attorney and president of the New Ellis Group in Princeton, New Jersey, Karen Kaplowitz discourages women from thinking there's a certain method for combining career and children. "Having it all is always a goal, not a formula."

Start with a cursory review of what gives you energy and what you simply can't bear. My friends and I have spent many hours dissecting the mind and body of the fulfilled stay-at-home mom, since most of us consider her the "perfect mother." We've also isolated the factors and characteristics that buoy women in the other two roles—that of full-time or part-time work outside the home. See which list best matches you and your situation:

Attributes of relatively happy stay-at-home moms

- A temperament suited to small children

- Financial means and a support network that works

- Faith- or value-driven desire to be at home

- Desire for major life change

- Easier hormonal/emotional adjustment

Attributes of relatively happy moms working outside the home
- Economic need

- High energy and good at handling stress

- Long-held desire to be a working mom

- Family-friendly job

- Need to restore herself, away from child

Attributes of relatively happy split-time moms:
- Adaptable personality

- More flexible budget

- Husband who's willing to help or meet his wife halfway

- Independent-minded and comfortable with lack of firm identity

Don't Force Yourself Into The Wrong Role!

The mistake many moms make is to force themselves into one of these roles—whether or not the lifestyle choice fits them or their postpartum persona. It's odd but we consider what's best for our kids and what's possible financially without focusing on our own temperaments and preferences.

You can't simply *be* a happy stay-at-home mom because you believe it's the right thing for your children. Exhaustion, husband resentment, or postpartum depression can interfere with your being the joyous full-time mom you dreamed you would be. Sometimes, too, women underestimate how much they'll despise the grunt work.

Nor can you ignore an out-of-nowhere panic about leaving a child in the hands of a stranger, even if your decision all along has been to go back to work. While it's natural to be nervous at first about a child-care provider, some moms find that they don't have the constitution they expected they would. We all have very individual thresholds and you can't *make* yourself comfortable with your company's day care, even if your officemate can't stop singing its praises.

Many times moms and dads find that small children make life infinitely more complicated. Part-time work meant to free you up to be a mommy, for example, can turn out to be full-time duties at half the pay. Or your offspring may make such a hysterical scene when you drop him at day care that you feel a scarlet M is emblazoned on your blouse.

Constant Adjustments

New moms have another dreaded adjustment: the almost constant need to reassess the elusive work/family balance and to meet the changing needs of the family. Before Baby came along, you knew your mind. You weighed your options, made your choices, and lived with them.

"I never had trouble making decisions before," says Gwen, a Texan friend of mine who's famously assertive. "Now I feel like I'm a quivering blob of indecision. Even if I make a stab at something certain, the kids get sick or my husband starts traveling or a commitment takes much more time than I planned. I'm constantly rehashing old decisions, and righting the balancing act that so frequently goes wrong."

The new you really does have a brain. It's just that your brain is taxed with a lot more considerations, many of them pressing because they involve the babe with whom you're besotted.

Oscar Wilde said "experience is the name we give to our mistakes." If you're fortunate enough to have choices about the amount of time you'll work or stay home, it's likely you'll initially let the pendulum swing too far in one direction and need to make adjustments.

Give yourself permission to be more fluid with decision making. Take a "day by day" approach or test-pilot a schedule or set of arrangements. Every good decision you'll make as a mom will largely be *by feel,* but that's likely to be a new facet to your personality since having children.

Ask, "Does This Fit My Child and My Family?"

Six months to two years into motherhood, you're likely to be far more attuned to your little one than you are to yourself. So this piece of advice will come easier: Be guided in making work arrangements—inside or outside the home—by your child's individual needs, personality, and development.

An interior designer I know had to quit her full-time job to pursue at-home freelance consulting because her infant son got sick too frequently, exposed to potent little germ-carriers at a clean but large child-care facility. Another mom I know took family leave from her job to hire a babysitter, after being dissatisfied with a child-care center's handling of a toddler vampire who all too often took a chunk out of her daughter.

Socialization may prove important to an overly clingy child you intended to have at home with you full-time for another year. And even the best researched schools and day care programs sometimes prove to be the wrong fit for certain kids. Siblings are different, too, one child managing well a hefty workweek away from Mom and Dad that a subsequent sibling's personality can't handle.

Demonstrate to child-care leaders and teachers that you're interested, involved and concerned. But ultimately, trust your own sense of your child's situations. Should you get a bad feeling, trust your deep reservoir of maternal intuition and make different arrangements.

Accept the Backup Plan

Duke was a rising star in his company when I got pregnant with our second son, Liam. But as was true with my first pregnancy, job crises waited to strike until I was full to bursting with child. Duke grew unhappy at work and discouraged about his prospects in a lousy economy. In his gloom, Duke was also gripped by anxiety over our increasing debt, which we had previously accepted as a side effect of the expensive preschool years. He told me, "I feel like I'm running on one of those wheels in a hamster's cage. I keep running faster and faster, but our family keeps falling further behind."

So, three months after having good-natured baby Liam, I started pounding the pavement for the elusive well-paying part-time or flexible work situation. I assumed I'd be granted this gem of a job, given my graduate school degree and my credentials as an accomplished woman and published writer. After nine months, though, I was forced to resort to back-up of the back-up plan. (Co-incidentally, this was about the time I stopped sending pithy notes about my accomplishments to my college alumni magazine.)

I accepted a full-time job in hospital marketing and public relations, the field that I had left triumphantly eight years before to pursue my lifelong dream—a full-time freelance writing career. I was devastated and angry. To quell the demons during my commute, I taped a message to the driver's-seat visor: "I chose this life." In other words, suck it up and do this for the sake of your family and your stressed-out husband.

Despite the burden of a fifty-hour-per-week job, my wonderful peers, creative work, and the constant drama of the hospital environment made a good home for me. Georgina, our loving nanny, tended to Patrick and Liam. Duke and I paid down the debt. And I wrung as much teaching, laughter, and snuggling as I could from the evening and weekend hours I was with my boys. As difficult as the back-up plan was for me, it bolstered my husband at a time he deeply needed bolstering, and the kids are not worse for wear. Three years of pent-up ideas now spring off my keyboard, Liam working next to me on his coloring books, enjoying having Mommy at home.

Every day, stay-at-home moms learn they cannot do everything on their own. They form coops with other moms to trade child care. Or hire part-time babysitters and cleaning people, dog-walkers and personal shoppers; get dinner and groceries delivered; and join gyms that provide child-care. Similarly, moms who work outside the home temper long-held ambitions, turn down promotions, and reject career-building projects or important work-related travel.

Making a change in plans feels to us like a giant admission of failure, because we have long envisioned how motherhood would look and feel, and how well we'd adjust to the blessings babies and children bring to our lives. But happy moms learn to reframe the situation, and view disappointments and missteps as needed steps in a long-term success strategy.

Like children, our progress often comes with two steps forward, one step back. Just know that sometimes a white hankie waved in the face of a maelstrom, can also be a way of moving on, growing up, and loving more.

As Much As Possible, Expel Guilt and Fear

Nagging guilt, doubt and fear are mothers' lifelong afflictions. You name it, we feel bad about it.

Jennifer from Cincinnati relates, "When I was a full-time stay-at-home mom, I felt guilty if I didn't take my kids to the playground often enough or didn't plan arts and crafts projects. Now that they're in preschool half-days so I can work from home, they play outside and do a craft everyday, but I feel guilty that they no longer have my undivided attention. I just can't seem to give myself a break from guilt."

Moms who choose to, or who must, work outside of family and home are tormented by the sickening feeling that they are lousy or selfish mothers. Guilt and shame thrive, despite research that finds that children receive only a half-hour less direct attention from working moms than moms busting their tails at home.

Overcompensating

Wanting her daughter to have all the perks a stay-at-home mother would have, a friend of mine who's a primary breadwinner registered her budding ingénue for a weeklong theater camp. Only problem was, the hours of the camp required my high-heeled friend to dash madly from work to day care to camp at 12:30 P.M., appear composed walking back into work, only to repeat that insane traffic pattern in reverse at 3:30 P.M.

Yet, I felt a tinge of sadness later, when she told me how much her admittedly high-maintenance daughter wants a day alone with Mom—to bake cookies and play dress-up. "I just have to schedule it, a day off, I mean," my friend said. Somehow, the notion of having to *schedule* cookies and dress-up amid our busy lives did seem wrong, and I understood all the more my friend's doggedness in compensating with a special theater camp.

The Dishes Can Wait

Author Ellen Gilchrist gives women writers two pieces of advice: "Fuck doubt. And the dishes can wait." Sometimes I want to strap a bullhorn to the top of my minivan and drive around the planned communities in San Diego, liberating moms from their guilt and their kitchens with this chant: F@#* doubt! And the dishes can wait!

We can only dispel guilt and doubt one at a time. Call out the irksome parasite and figure out exactly what you're afraid of or worried about. Ask, Is this a rational feeling? Is there evidence to support my self-criticism or doubt? Who or what introduced this notion to me and is this a credible source? Will I care, or will my child care, about this matter a year from now, or ten years from now? How does this problem fit into the overall scheme of the beliefs and mission of our family?

Talk out dilemmas with friends and with your kids. The more you share your angst, the more your spouse and your family will understand the pressures you're under and how they can help.

Bad Guilt, Good Guilt

Remind yourself that motherhood is a subjective and personal matter, about which society has unmanageable and ridiculous expectations. Then, throw off the bear on your back. Expel the vast majority of your self-doubt. Be a trailblazer, and demonstrate that great families are garnered a gazillion different ways.

Some guilt you'll never outgrow, or talk yourself out of. For whatever reason, those doubts have special clout so they can serve as needle indicators of times when your priorities or life balance gets out of whack.

Try to avoid wearing the catastrophic lenses brought on, for example, by being a control freak, or premenstrual. Don't let dirty dishes, late library books, forgotten appointments, and brown lawns say volumes to you about your life.

Life is too fast-moving. Statements kids make are too amazing and insightful. Don't squander your already paltry energy on dirty dishes or unfounded doubts.

chapter six

Wife, Mom, and Leftovers of Me

Dealing with the Personality Drain of Motherhood

> **SECRET:** *Moms lose a sense of self but amass life meaning in spades.*

❀ "I'm afraid I'm not even going to recognize you in another year," said my close friend Carole Lynn, who lives in a magnificent flat in San Francisco, full of vintage furniture finds and one-of-a-kinds she picked up in Paris flea markets while working abroad. Carole Lynn has not yet married or had children, but she has long been a soul mate. Nevertheless, she couldn't help but be shocked that over a short span of motherhood, my spirit was shaken, my chins doubled, my children had become the center of my guilt- and anxiety-ridden universe, and my writing aspirations sidelined.

Her prognosis reverberated through me hundreds of times in upcoming weeks and months: Will I recognize you before long? Will any of your distinguishing qualities remain when motherhood is finished riding roughshod over you and your dreams? I was seared by her observations, in part because she called forth fears I had hoped were baseless, and in part because the metamorphosis

I was experiencing seemed unavoidable and, to a great extent, healthy for both me and my family.

Welcome to the identity crisis of early motherhood! If you waited till your thirties to have children, you thought you were immune to the personality enema for which motherhood is famous. You expected a change in character, not a shakedown. But it turns out motherhood packs a punch for all of us, regardless of age, perky innocence or weathered professionalism, high school smarts or forty-something wisdom.

Early Midlife Crisis?

In their book *Midlife Crisis at 30,* authors Lia Macko and Kerry Rubin detail why American women—with or without children—are experiencing emotional upheaval and painful inner crossroads two decades before our mothers traditionally did. With women staying single longer and not becoming mothers till later, there's "an entirely new set of circumstances that compress the decisions about marriage, children, and earning power into a very narrow window," Macko explains. "Women of our generation are hitting these conflicts for the first time in their thirties whereas in past generations, it was a slow burn."

Today's thirty-five- to forty-five-year-olds are rushing to get everything in, which is why wedding invitations from friends are often so quickly followed by birth announcements. And why many of us are dizzy from implications of decisions we had little time to consider. I asked Christine D'Amico, a life coach and the author of *The Pregnant Woman's Companion,* how smart women can be so dumb when it comes to predicting the life overhaul parenthood brings. "Many women deciding to have children today have little exposure to young families, except what we see in the media. On TV and in magazines, having a child looks so romantic, beautiful, and clean. Not to mention it's been ten years since most of us babysat. And who has time to research that far ahead? All we can manage is to study up on getting pregnant and delivering the baby."

Deciding "it's now or never," moms today signal their acceptance of dramatic life change only by running headlong into deadlines. As for our identities, we want children but we don't want to be dragged behind the speeding chariot of family life until our features are indistinguishable. Life change, bring it on but don't mess with our already well-honed souls.

Soon, though, the velocity of loving and caring for small brutes makes it impossible for us to keep the metamorphosis of motherhood at bay. Before long, we loosen our grip voluntarily because as threatened as we feel, we want to embrace our little loved ones with both arms—with all of us.

Different Takes on Identity

Not every mom wriggles so in the net. Some moms welcome a new identity, tired of their old ones or from trying to find one. Others are simply *ready*. Single and career-driven till she was thirty-one, married at thirty-five, and a first-time mom at thirty-six, Orange County mom Pam doesn't have any nostalgia for her premarital independence. "As trite as it sounds, I felt I found my life purpose when my baby was born."

Aimee, a thirtysomething physician's assistant, sat next to Pam at one of my mommy tell-all sessions. Aimee had a very different experience, having met her husband at twenty-one and starting their family quickly afterward. "If we had waited until my career was established, I don't know that I would have survived mother-hood. If you haven't had much, you're not giving up as much."

In contrast, a woman in her forties broke down and cried when she described the changes to marriage first-time parenthood had wrought. "We can't even have dinner together anymore," the woman sobbed. "We used to cook together and have a glass of wine." To which Aimee says, "I think it's better to be unformed, not to know so well what you like before children take it away from you."

Some moms, like Gayle in the Berkshires of Massachusetts, are so accustomed to juggling several personas that they allow mother-hood to broaden their self-definition more naturally. "I was wild and dated a lot of men in college. But at the same time I was very spiritual and sang in church choirs. Because I already had a bunch of identities, I just added mom to the mix. I can be a mother and still be sexual. I can be an at-home mom and an intellectual."

Adapt—Huh?

Why is adaptation hard for some of us? Orlean, the character Meryl Streep plays in the quirky feature film *Adaptation,* notes that orchids are asexual, having made the ultimate adjustment to the environment to survive. Orlean asks why people admire adaptation in animals and plants but abhor it in themselves.

In the classic book *The Lonely Crowd: A Study of the Changing American Culture,* the late Yale professor David Riesman explains that societal personalities change as national economies do. In-stead of growing up with a strict internal code to guide our behav-ior as previous generations of Americans did, our character in the communications age is *externally* guided, melded by the deluge of information we receive every day about what is smart, cool, and successful. The result: We all try to cultivate quirky personalities and somehow still wind up having the same preferences and eccentricities as countless others in our demographic group.

I was brought up by '60s mind-set parents who prized dissident behavior for the good of the planet. Only, it turns out I'm a big cliché: the Dodge Grand Caravan–driving and George Foreman grill-buying daughter of former Vietnam War protestors who now have IRA's, shop at Costco, and religiously watch *Law and Order*.

Duke and I are still stunned by this fact: that our desire for an unconventional life makes us conventional. Having spent more than a decade single prior to settling down, I learned, like Carrie Bradshaw from *Sex and the City,* how to command attention in a room full of people. I aspired like Diane Keaton in *Baby Boom* to join with other entrepreneurial moms—playpens nearby—and achieve trailblazing success, furthering the cause of creative parenting solutions. But mostly, I found that having children made me less visible to a world I used to dominate, and scrambling to lead the pack when working-mom alternatives were limited or unfeasible.

Aging and Fading

Sure, some lessons were inevitable as I grew older. Didn't I *have* to fade to allow the next generation to pop forward? Carrie and the *Sex and the City* girls had to grow up, face breast cancer and infertility, and settle into long-term relationships.

Fading is one thing but suppressing is quite another. Child-care experts tell us to relent to all our youngsters' needs—without regard to our own authenticity or personality. The irrefutable needs of children, not to mention the style points assessed by intensive mothering, demand that we stay at home, use top-quality day care only certain hours per week, and devote a precise portion of our day to molding vegetables into enticing animal shapes and making puppets from Kleenex. As if we didn't already feel like robots, wearing grooves in our hardwoods, shuttling back and forth between table and dishwasher, between living room and toy shelf!

Soul Solutions

How will you express yourself in a robot's shell? How will you defy expectations, if all your decisions are already scripted by a marketing plan? Will any of your cherished idiosyncrasies survive the adaptation wringer?

This is what fellow robo-moms have to say:

Let Go

The Buddhist teacher and author Joseph Goldstein says we experience "mental rope burn" when we cling to people, possessions, and even to our self-concept. We think that by clinging, we can ford the stream of change. We also confuse attachment with love, believing that to love anyone and anything including ourselves, we must hold on for dear life.

Chasing Your Groove

Rachel, one of my dearest friends, works part-time at home as a marketing consultant and according to my calculations, another sixty hours per week as Wonder Woman. She's a loving mother to two boys; loving spouse; manager of her psychiatrist husband's practice; attentive friend and neighbor who checks in with her circle a couple times a week, offering play dates, casseroles, Starbucks, and a listening ear; hostess of Shabbat dinners and Jewish holiday meals to which at least twenty people are always expected; and take-charge volunteer coordinator of maybe ten events per year ranging from school auctions and fund-raisers that bring in a half-million philanthropic dollars in a night. Her energy surges past the rest of us tortoises—even given her husband's extensive travel schedule, her young sons' frequent colds and sleep difficulties, and the snags all of us experience in our bottlenecked lives.

Rachel is happiest, she tells her friends, "in her groove." In this hyper-efficient mode, she will, for example, buy soy burgers while fielding questions on her cell phone from a board of directors in Houston. Unfortunately, her groove frequently sneaks off her slender frame and bounces off the walls, like Peter Pan's shadow, or a laser pointer with Tourette's. Every day Rachel tries to recapture her groove, double her points by meeting friends for coffee *and* walks, or grocery shopping only when her nanny is there to put the items away so she has time to play with her kids.

Like Rachel, many new moms chase the past: your former self's sunny disposition, your wedding day weight, your premarital libido, the energy of your younger years, or the independence of your single days. We just don't understand why life is so hard these days, why we're so mentally sluggish and prone to illness, and why we are snappish and irritable when we never were that way before.

My mom recently said to me, "We miss the old Marg, the one who used to laugh so hard and so long." At first, I was devastated, thinking, "She sees what I see: that I'm not as fun anymore, and that the stress of motherhood has permanently marred me." A few hours later, my sister, Catherine, also the mother of two young boys, slapped sense into me: "Mom has just forgotten how difficult it can be with two little ones at home. You're still laughing, Marg, but now you appreciate very dark jokes, jokes that are only funny to the damned—and mothers of small children."

Lose Yourself to Find Yourself

Instead of fretting that your humor's been carted away by trolls, along with your brain and clitoris, my wisest mommy friends have decided to get into the pushcart and let the ride take them where it will. They've stopped waking up every morning, rebuking themselves for not being what they were before, and have instead, gasp, let their identities be scrambled up like their morning eggs. As a therapist suggested the first time—and potentially last, given her advice—I met with her, "You've got to lose yourself to find yourself."

I was in no mood for a confusing Jesus parable, mind you, in the midst of first-year motherhood self-obliteration. Had I not just written an entire three hundred-page book about how it was entirely possible for modern women to retain thriving personas as they settled into and learned the ropes of marriage?! One last nail in her coffin, my counselor remarked, "After all, it's inevitable that new mothers lose their identity."

I know blasphemy at $100 per hour when I hear it. Only the notion that "finding yourself" might be a by-product of losing yourself pestered me over the subsequent muddled weeks. Could there be some benefit to "letting go" in a passage of life that so far appeared utterly out of control? I decided to devote another year of counseling to find out.

Surrender Control

Much brighter students figured this out unaided, and earlier: Stop pretending to be in charge, and let your new, cuddly charge lead the way. Let your baby transport you to vulnerable, scary, and unfathomably joyful destinations. Abandon your definitions of success and mastery, and experience instead the quickly passing days in which your juice-moustache beauty looks at you with complete adoration.

You can do it, too. Go to a bridge in your town, and dump the ashes of your beloved former self over the side. Then feed the ducks, or show your three-year-old son how to skip a rock. Be exhausted from telling him not to climb on the railing. Drive home with low blood sugar, giving yourself a pep talk for getting through lunch and to nap time without yelling or spanking.

Above all, do not await the phoenix because in the baby and toddler years of motherhood, rebirth comes like molasses. Glints of your new identity will flap around you. But don't bother trying to catch them because their disparate shiny feathers are being configured somewhere beyond your control.

Go Ahead and Grieve

It's all right to cry, and even better to scream. If you're having a midlife crisis, this may be your one shot in ninety years for intense self-pity and excruciating contemplation. And the longer you tell yourself you *should* be happy, the greater the chance that you'll become the family doormat or the lively hostess who spews resentments the later it gets and the more she drinks.

For some reason, our generation of moms internalizes the major life questions that previous generations took to protest marches and to the political arena. Instead of burning bras, or blaming society and its heaped-too-high expectations of mothers, we blame ourselves.

In guilty silence and sometimes unspeakable pain, we regret having a child, a botched birth, multiple births, or a boy when we wanted a girl. The coming of a little one can summon the pain of a miscarriage or a family member's passing. Yet, moms think even garden-variety sadness is on the "what not to wear" list, and believe there is something wrong with them if they don't feel ecstatic all the time.

Worse yet, we call ourselves freaks for having normal reactions and mixed feelings to such enormous life stress. "I feel I have to lie and say I love motherhood so no one thinks I'm a freakishly bad mother," says a mom in North Carolina. A new stepmother in New York City, confesses, "I'm a monster sometimes, when I compete with my stepdaughter for my husband's attention. A good mother doesn't act that way."

Moms who believe deep down that they are bad mothers are caught in a vicious cycle. The more they admit feelings of disappointment or loss, of uncontrollable rage or relentless anxiety, the more estranged they feel from motherhood. Holding back their rage or sadness becomes as hopeless as trying to fend off quickening contractions.

Let the Tears Begin

The last month of my pregnancy with Patrick, I completed a year's work on the *What No One Tells the Bride* manuscript, sent the package to my publisher, and started nonstop wailing. Buying Nicolette Larson's lullaby cassette inspired full-body sobs. Childbirth scenes on TV shows caused moaning torrents of tears. Stepping into the baby's nursery brought on a more cathartic hoohooing, so I'd sit in the glider, massage my tummy, and rock myself for hours.

Two important lessons materialized from my monthlong bawling fest. One, it's not advisable to finish a marathon of writing and experience post-project depression while on the verge of losing one's mucus plug. More far-reaching, however, was lesson two: that in order to be reborn, all of us must pass through a tunnel of tears.

What a magnificent catch-up job my body did, forcing me to mourn the fact of having been given up as a newborn, after thirty-three years of largely avoiding the painful aspects of my birth and adoption. In essence, my brain and the hormones preparing me for childbirth demanded that I enter a canal of seemingly unrelenting pain and sadness to reach the other side.

I was on a schedule, mind you, giving myself a month to wrap up my single most important career accomplishment before embarking on my single most important life accomplishment, that of bringing Patrick, and later his enchanting brother, Liam, into the world. Shockingly, the Auto-Pilot of New Life had her own timing, emptying closets of skeletons, exposing letters hidden in lingerie drawers, clearing the haunted way for defiant, broad-shouldered love to emerge.

So it is with all mothers, and all human beings. As Anne Lamott wrote in a column, "Breaking the Surface," for the website *Salon*: "[The process of breaking the surface] is about the willingness or necessity of being wiped out of what you think holds you together, to face a benevolent annihilation, without all the stuff you think defines you, the stuff where we live, which we think is reality."

Give Yourself a Mourning Period

Okay, so maybe I'm scaring you silly with these dark scenarios. But deep down are fears you need to face, lest your psychic-from-birth and soon-to-be-verbal offspring call them out. You well-read mommies know I'm preaching emotional intelligence—an honesty about and willingness to permit all feelings—which we're supposed to teach our kids. To Ethan, the loss of a *Bob the Builder* backpack is devastating, and child-care experts advise us not to minimize or brush off his experience of pain. Only most of us have plenty of work to do getting emotionally intelligent about the black-and-blue state of our own affairs since motherhood delivered its wallop.

The break-out album of our childhoods was Marlo Thomas's *Free to Be You and Me*. On it, the hulking football star Rosey Grier crooned "It's All Right to Cry" to the next generation of potentially emotionally stunted boys. Yet, it's turned out that most of the stoics

I know are women, mothers who go to the well again and again for stamina to serve others, only to find the well eventually runs dry.

So, new moms, give yourselves a mourning period, snippets of time in which you submerge yourself in the feelings you feel, raw as they may be. Get away with your spouse for a weekend and grieve the former lives and luxuries you enjoyed, even as you marvel at the way baby Beatrice waddles or comment on how blown away you were that four-year-old Zach knew what a rhyme was.

Make lists of all the things you've learned, as parents, to live without: holding hands instead of pushing a stroller. Reading the paper over coffee. Lingering in art galleries. Walking across town. Looking made-up and pulled together in public. Going to a movie or having sex on a whim. Simmering homemade tomato sauce for hours. Small purses, clipped recipes, alone time in the bathroom, impulsive spending, and driving alone with the windows rolled down.

In the same way you cart photos of your kids around, carry with you little symbols of your loss. If you miss being spontaneous, carry a little confetti around in your coin purse. If you miss time with your girlfriends, they deserve a photo in your wallet, too. In this way, you observe and acknowledge the sacrifices you've made the same way you honor the cutie-patooties who have expanded your heart.

Keep your wedding photos visible, even if they remind you of how buff you once were as bride and groom. Keep the aura of your iconoclast selves alive in your home, and talk with your child about the days before he came along, which he will love hearing.

Feel Blue Sometimes

Instead of feeling guilty for feeling blue, just feel blue now and then. Motherhood is the most demanding job you'll ever have, and acknowledging its enormous drain on you is not the same thing as regretting having brought children onto this green earth. After all, how will your kids learn compassion without being in the presence of pain? How will they know it's safe to tell you terrible or frightening things if you gloss over or dodge your less attractive emotions?

Make it safe for everyone to feel, not wallow, but touch and taste real-life reactions. Other than cutting yourself off from emotions altogether and from the delightful and exhilarating moments in which—shazam!—motherhood is fulfilling and magical, facing the putrid stuff is your only path to reconciliation.

Go On with the New You

Patrick, now a second grader, says I'm supposed to update my seventies lingo, and use terms like *fly* and *bling bling*. But when I think about the resurfacing of a mother's ego, for some reason leisure suits, afros, and strutting one's stuff come to mind. Go *on* with your bad self.

Most moms said they began to feel vaguely human again three years after adding a child to their lives. That's what the brain research indicates, too, that moms' mental capacities return to pre-pregnancy states and then some three years into motherhood.

Once your upstart goes off to preschool and later kindergarten, you can sew maybe one, two at the most, personal interests or aspirations into your life. Psychologists say that a mother needs only carry threads of her self-image through the wild, plaid weave of motherhood. So that a couple decades from now, when your boomerang college grads leave the nest for good, you can start whipping stitches like a banshee, darning a new you.

Don't Vanish into Motherhood

Some moms lose themselves in their kids, identify too closely with Isabel and Dylan, and measure themselves by the successes and failures of their gene pool. Teresa, the school counselor who personally experienced the hardships of postpartum depression, says the moms who can't seem to break away are often the ones who never dealt with the emotional issues of this giant transition to motherhood. Instead of acknowledging the dual pulls within, they threw themselves at a single target, hoping to quiet the ceaseless agitation they felt inside.

Single-target moms and dads of the opposite ilk also weeble, wobble, and fall down. Duke and I know a handsome, blond-haired six-year-old whose parents have all but abandoned to the care of others to pursue dual careers, worldwide travel, and fruits of a mon-eyed adult life. Meanwhile, their not-so-little boy soils himself at sleepovers, and already takes prescription medication for migraines.

Sit Down and Seize the Day

Duke cannot cope with the idea that for the next twenty years, he has to accept a diminished quality of life in which his appetite for a full and interesting life is constantly in conflict with his commitment to being a responsible, loving father. I am strangely soothed by it, the idea that the Me of Olden Days will return decades from now, colored by all the experiences I've had, from finger painting in the back-yard to waiting for my boys to come home from high school games and parties.

I also deeply believe people should not put off until tomorrow what they could do today. As a child, I visited sick and dying parish-ioners in the hospital with my dad, a Presbyterian minister. My jobs in hospital public relations ensured that I had eight years in which to work near dialysis and chemotherapy treatment rooms, and to be reminded each day that I had to live life to the fullest.

This is undoubtedly why it was difficult for me to "lay fallow" like a farmer's resting field, putting off my growing season for that of my children. Having seen too many lives slapped by fate, and too many people taken away senselessly, the notion of carpe diem, "Seize the day," badgers me constantly. Perhaps you know, too, how frightening it is to have parents retire and almost immediately encounter health setbacks and cancers. So that life and all the joys we want to reap from it, feel even more condensed.

Most of the moms with whom I'm close feel this ping-pong game inside, a volley of "Pay attention to this precious, fast-moving time with your babies" that's met and returned with "Life is too short to keep denying myself new lessons and new passions." One of the hardest things to get used to, as a new mom, is this constant ricochet of emotions, equal tugs of adoring our kids and craving our own thoughts and pursuits. I figured eventually I'd stop feeling like Dr. Doolittle's two-headed llama, and concede to one leader or another.

Yet talking with seasoned moms and therapists, I have learned that the agitation never goes away entirely. As long as we live, whether we're absorbed in raising a brood or thinking about them from afar, the engrained motion of mothering continues. Five years since I've had a newborn, I still catch myself, at cocktail parties or in conversations with colleagues, swaying back and forth on my feet—the stance of a mother rocking a baby.

As threatening as it feels, you will emerge from early parenthood a changed woman. Like Eric Carle's wonderfully illustrated children's book *The Very Hungry Caterpillar,* your new wings will contain the colors and shapes of all the pizzas you ate late at night in college. All the shades of Burgundy and Chardonnay you once consumed at romantic dinners and winery tours. All the gold of medals and résumés you acquired before children entwined themselves around you, body and soul. But the arrangement of the hues, the spikes and twirls of design, the precise size and span of the wings is, splendidly, not up to you.

A few years from now when I emerge as a new mariposa, I'm convinced that my dear friend Carole Lynn will recognize me. She'll recognize my fortitude, and admire the life meaning I've amassed in the teetering act of combining motherhood with self-expression. I'll be me throughout, but like a sauce that's been reduced to its finest, most potent flavor, I'll have surrendered excesses. Seemingly diminished, in essence I will have gained strength.

Disappointments Motherhood Brings

"Motherhood brings out the worst in me. I never knew I could yell, hit, or get as frustrated as I do."

"I feel like a slave. It's nonstop work."

"My children are really mean to me sometimes. I had no idea kids could be so hateful."

"I never get time alone with my husband. I miss the couple we were before we had kids."

"I used to be so efficient. Now I'm at home and I *still* can't stay on top of everything."

"Just when I get good at a stage, my son changes and I have to start all over again, trying out new skills."

"I feel guilty about working, even though I love my work."

"We have so much less money and flexibility."

"I hate that dads get off so easy, while moms are in charge of everything."

"I don't have time to take care of my health."

Pleasant Surprises Motherhood Brings

"I had heard it was going to be awful. But my husband and I love being parents."

"How much easier it is to make friends! With moms, you instantly have something in common."

"Labor and delivery, just six hours with no drugs, wasn't nearly as bad as I expected. It was an awesome experience."

"I didn't expect to find it so fulfilling. Secretly, I like it much more than my work."

"My in-laws treat me better—with greater respect. Maybe because I'm the gatekeeper to their grandchildren!"

"I thought motherhood would change me as an individual. While I have to work at keeping my identity, it is doable."

"Having less money, I actually get such a kick out of deep-bargain shopping. Marshall's is high-end for me now!"

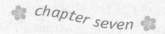

My Mother's in the Mirror

Unpacking Family Baggage and Launching Your New Family

> SECRET: *To grow great families, mothers need to feel connected—to others and to the divine.*

Legendary among pilots is a story revealed on a black box, or cockpit voice recorder, recovered from the site of a Middle Eastern plane crash. On it was a recording of the poignant and private final minutes in which the pilot realized a cabin fire at the back of the plane would doom the flight. The tape revealed that the pilot spent his final seconds singing to himself. Hurtling to the earth, he didn't pick a religious hymn or a love song. His voice quavered out the words of the lullaby his mother sang to him as a child.

My mother's lullabies were reborn in me, too, the first days I held my newborn Patrick. For decades I had not thought about the song my mom made up to sing to my sister and me. "Mommy loves Patrick and Patrick loves Mommy, Daddy loves Patrick and Patrick loves Daddy . . . We all love each other, how happy we are"—the words, melody and all, rose from my heart and into my pipes spontaneously. Strangely, traditions of my childhood I thought were buried in boxes in an attic proved ready-to-wear once I was a mom.

Like I have, most of you probably cut the cord from your childhood home years ago. You did your time in therapy or in family feuds and moved beyond blaming your parents for your various shortcomings. But parenthood—and the arrival of your parents' grandchildren—bind you anew to your family of origin, all its quirks and calamities. This period in your life can feel like regression or it can feel like coming home. Nonetheless, there are some bellwethers my mommy friends and I can tell you about, as well as some fine lines we've learned to tiptoe in our relations with flesh and blood and with in-laws.

Babies Are Healers

First, the good news: Babies are tiny shaman, able to repair and soothe contentious relationships within families the way few other things can. Kid-lee-winks, as my grandmother used to call us, are equally good for close families, letting off steam when the closeness gets a tad overwhelming. At the least, our gorgeous progeny become a buffer—a ready conversation topic—replacing family dialogues that used to veer toward politics, religion, or the exorbitant cost of the house we just bought. Folks are generally more reluctant to argue in front of children, too, inspiring grown-ups to act like grown-ups because tots are present.

Conversations with kids around are usually brief, full of distractions and interruptions, and accordingly superficial. You can't get into too much trouble with your anarchist sister-in-law if you stick to talking about fifteen-minute dinner recipes or serve as the spotter to your niece's lawn somersaults. You've still got to dodge rapid-fire advice from mothers and mothers-in-law but in general, kids' naps, feeding times, stomachaches, runny noses, swim lessons, soccer practices, field trips, and sleepovers give you ample "get out of family functions free" cards.

Early parenthood is universally traumatic and therefore, a great equalizer among family members. A friend of mine described the awkward gulf that used to exist between her and her sisters-in-law who hadn't attended college or lived on their own before getting married as she had. Come the birth of her children though, that gulf was filled with shared interests: of how to get babies to sleep and husbands to help. Similarly, my parents and sister are far more comfortable with paper napkins and takeout than they were with holidays I drenched in cream sauces, handmade place cards, and fresh cranberry wreaths I stayed up till three in the morning finishing.

As new parents, you're needy and vulnerable, which makes you very accessible to previously resentful or detached relatives. Tracy Thompson wrote in *Lifetime* magazine about having severed all ties with older sister Ellen Wright after a lifetime of bitter sibling rivalry and competition. Yet, six weeks after Tracy gave birth to her daughter Emma, she descended into a postpartum depression that made her pick up the phone and, in desperation, call her sister for help. "My husband was scared, his nearby family was doing all they could and we had run out of money for child care."

Ellen got on the next flight to come to her sister's aid. When Ellen arrived and took baby Emma into her arms, Tracy realized that "at last we had something in common besides this stupid, decades-old competition." Indeed, Tracy says, "In every life, there ought to be somebody you can go back to, a person who is of your blood in a way not even a husband is, someone who personifies the earliest concept of 'home.'"

At a mommy "tell-all" I hosted one night over wine and

cheesecake, Gina told her own story of reconciliation. When Gina was in college, her mother graduated from bridge and Bingo to a full-fledged gambling addiction played out in Atlantic City. Indeed, Mom's gambling debts led to Gina's family losing their home, Gina's tuition money, everything. Yet fifteen years, a marriage, and two children later, Gina is happy watching her aging mother and kindergarten-aged daughter together. "Especially because my mother's health is not great, I want Allison to spend as much time with her as she can."

A signal of how far Gina's come, she can allow a relationship to develop, a grandmother's love to take root, unsullied by the terrible shame and betrayal Gina experienced with her mom. Many of us in the room shared Gina's sentiment—that the rapport between our children and their grandparents is sacred—and on a different plane than our own interactions with parents. I have no problem when the boys miss church to do breakfast with their grandpa. Stories their grandpa tells over pancakes drenched in boysenberry syrup are holy, too.

Of course, healing is not always possible or desirable. A recovering alcoholic who stopped drinking when she became a mother, Lola considers her mother a central culprit in her troubled past. "I now *intimately* understand what my mother went through. I also understand that she had a choice of how to treat us, because I make those choices every day. To me, that makes her all the more despicable."

Discovering Your Mommy Leverage

Fortunately, the second development that comes with being the recipient, not just the giver, of gifts on Mother's Day is that you gain "Mommy Leverage." Since this is about the only addition in influence (in a sea of lost control and plundered respect) moms acquire, it's important that you wield this clout with a vengeance.

When Jennifer's obnoxious, snobby in-laws moved from Northern California to San Diego to be closer to their grandchildren, my mompool was quick to remind Jennifer of her powers. First we persuaded her that even pretentious relatives are perfectly acceptable—and free!—child-care providers. To ease her resentment of increased in-law presence in her life, we encouraged Jennifer to impose upon Witchy-poo for babysitting. Ultimately, we advised, you "play the game" with your relations and tune out contemptible remarks and suggestions to keep the hope alive of hotel room service and weekends away with your husband.

We also encouraged Jennifer to manage kinfolk logistics to suit herself, for example, by limiting visits to Grandma's house of breakables and insisting that the children function best in their own childproofed environment. Use the junior member of your clan as a ready excuse so visits stay short and sweet, pop-in arrivals are frowned upon, gifts are educational and nonviolent, smoking stays outside, unwanted get-togethers get cancelled, and school programs and dance recitals take up the time you'd otherwise spend being dumped upon by your mother or his mother.

Because you control access to Princess Becky and Future Quarterback Devon, meddling grandparents can often be tamed. The strongest message you can send your crusty father-in-law, when he insists you use corporal punishment on your out-of-line three-year-old, is to stop issuing invitations and stop including him in your plans.

There are, however, several ways in which Mommy Leverage gets diluted. Many of us who are financially strapped from one spouse not working or from paying expensive nursery school bills make the mistake of borrowing or accepting money from our parents or in-laws. It's also true that as your parents worship and spoil the grandkids, you may realize and greatly resent that you were not nearly as well coddled as a child. Sometimes, too, grandmothers gloat about "payback time" in which you are now the victim of rolled eyes, talking back, and "C'mon, Mom" whines you once perpetrated on her.

Kids Dredge up the Past

This brings us to the third by-product of babies on views of your lineage. Having kids dredges everything up, the same way a toddler unearths lost action figures, Barbie shoes, or week-old half-eaten Gogurt from the depths of a sandbox. Parenthood triggers reactions in us, flashes and twitches steeped in family history and the dysfunction that reigned there. As new moms and dads, we're often blindsided by feelings about incidents and rituals we didn't even know we remembered. Some sweet, others painful, mental snapshots of ourselves as children now appear with far greater relevance and meaning.

Our mother's expressions worm their way into our mouths. Bygones such as "Because I said so!" and "Do I have to stop this car?" belong in the Smithsonian, not in your vernacular. Yet, if you're like most moms, your past is as active in your daily life as your children are, the sticky fingers of history leaving distinct marks on your expectations and choices.

Counselors Rick and Jan Hanson, who wrote the book *Mother Nurture,* suggest we try to sort intense, young reactions from the more moderate, here-and-now ones, letting go of the deepest part of our distress. If you're like me, you barely have enough time to locate the spots on the bathroom walls where your recently potty-trained child wiped poop off his fingers, so childhood dilemmas fall to the bottom of the mulling list. As does a groomed inner awareness that would allow you to separate childhood apparitions from the current feelings of guilt, agitation, and rage that have recently sunk into bean bags and made themselves at home in your life.

Still, because women in their thirties and forties are very susceptible to depression, you cannot afford to dismiss these hard tasks of sorting through your emotional trash bags. However puny it may be, you do have to have an inner life, a sense of your own spirit.

When dicey memories or curiously strong instincts are dredged up, you've got to connect with moms and other nurturers who can help you sort it out. Anne Lamott, my favorite mother writer and the author of *Operating Instructions,* writes in a "Letter to a Pregnant Friend" published on the website *Salon:*

> You will not want to tell most people how wasted and crazy you feel sometimes, because you do not want them to think that you are a broken cuckoo clock of a parent. But you probably are. We all are; mad as fucking hatters, to use the psychological term. And raising a child is like pouring Miracle-Gro on all your fears and character defects, so you have to talk about what's real, with safe people. Otherwise you are going to feel so isolated and deficient that it will damage your spirit.

Let us help you begin lacing a minuscule inner life. From love-filled to abuse-ridden childhoods, my friends and I offer a few important tips for maneuvering memory lane and forging new memories for your brand-new family.

Feel Connected

No mom I've met ever complains about this aspect of mother-hood: being a part of a secret society of women who know the height and depth of a mother's love and sacrifices. Caring about even the small turns of your child's life, and living in constant fear of your child being taken or hurt, you are *every* mother—from the Virgin Mary to Peter Rabbit's beside-herself mom. You are Sophie of the Meryl Streep movie *Sophie's Choice* and the stranger at Costco who waves knowingly, after waiting for your parking space through the unloading of diapers and juice boxes, and extended buckling of squirming limbs into their car seats. We are all con-nected, perhaps by the strand of saliva we are so quick to apply to chocolate on our children's chins.

The Circle of Life

What no one tells the mom is how powerful a role the "circle of life" plays in parenthood, and I don't just mean the number of times you're subjected to *The Lion King* sound track. As evolved as we think we are, primal urges and your links to the past become in-creasingly germane the longer you're a parent.

Outside the rhino exhibit at the zoo, two-year-old Liam offered his interpretation of muddy nuzzling: "Baby wants his mama." At the nearby monkey habitat, where a furry tike leaped among tree limbs and shrieked frantically, Liam explained, "He can't find his mama." The totality of Liam's worldview, and of the natural order of all things, relied on one relationship—that between a mother and child.

Having been adopted at birth by parents I know as Mom and Dad, I spent thirty-five years downplaying the role of nature in my life. I was a virtual twin to my sister, whom my adoptive mom bore thirteen months after adopting me. Blonde hair and blue eyes was all the DNA I needed.

With such extraordinarily caring parents, I made up a story in first grade to explain adoption to myself: "The lady who gave birth to me was sick and could not take care of me so I went to live with the Starks, who wanted a baby very, very much." That wasn't the truth but without the details at six years old, I preferred to close the door on my adoption story. My life as part of a loving, happy family was already complete and I was wholly satisfied having the straightforward family demographics of my peers.

Yet, thirty years later, having done what mammals do and carried growing babies within me, the door to my past creaked open. I learned that newborns know their mommies' voices from the womb. Unmistakably then, I was compelled to see my nature the way Liam did: The baby is crying for his mama. The baby is looking for his mama.

Having been blessed with a wonderful counselor, I had a guide to help me separate the taffy strands of my emerging depression. Questions about my birth and birth mother arose because I was experiencing a crisis in identity typical of early motherhood, about which we talked extensively in the previous chapter. I was one lost mommy, amid the strains of demanding babies, oscillating hormones, a high-jacked writing career, and a husband having a career, and thus, mid-life crisis. Within months, I found, talked to, and eventually was reunited with my birth mother and my sons' bloodline grandmother.

It wasn't easy. My sister was hurt that the boundless love and affection with which we were raised were "not enough" for me. And upon meeting and staring at each other for likenesses, both my birth mom and I had to rush to the bathroom with stomach distress.

My birth mom has not had subsequent children and was struggling with a depression of her own when I introduced my broken self and my ray-of-light babies to her. I was the product of a relationship with a man she loved who turned out to be married. Yet, she later said, I was the accomplishment in life of which she was most proud—the baby she carried and enabled to go on to great life and loves. Four years later, we continue to get to know one another and make up for birthdays and Mother's Days that transpired before we met.

While the connection I forged is more remarkable than some, all new mothers get pulled back into a familial stew. Comparisons to your mom are inevitable, if not always welcome.

Our Spouses' Demons

Bless their souls, partners and husbands also have to deal with flashbacks. It pains Duke to recall his preschool and early grade school years—a time in which he was fought over, kidnapped, and disappointed by parents who were getting divorced and bitterly angry at one another. Therapy is not his bag, nor is he necessarily conscious of times in which our family life evokes his past.

Yet, when I make arrangements for our boys' birthday parties—which might more properly be termed extravaganzas because of the lengths to which I go—Duke can't help but feel slighted. He quietly mentions, "I never really had birthday parties."

Similarly, he signed up for Indian Guides with Patrick in spite of my concerns about overscheduling the family. Duke explained, "I had to quit Scouting when I was young because it fell on the night my dad called me at my mom's house."

I liken Duke's experience to that of leeches used even today to knit tiny blood vessels back together after microsurgery. You refuse to let terrible memories suck any more strength from you and believe sufficient healing has transpired. But deep down, mending is still needed because children, and our handling of them, expose even our tiniest wounds. Let those little bleeds remain and you're likely to taint the whole family with anger and pain.

True, some of you are better off distancing yourselves from the abysmal origins of your first family. You are fueled by a desire to parent well in spite of having had poor examples. But sometimes, when you feel safe enough, you can allow even the worst memories to bring you little snatches of wisdom. You can pull from a bad scene the hint that someone tried to do the right thing. And you'll get reacquainted with your own innocence.

Loving with abandon, without fear of pain or price, is a gift our toddlers and preschoolers give us every day. Identify with the part of you that loved this way once, and you'll put into a tender context your needy child's tired tantrums and clamors for attention. See yourself in them and you'll have greater strength for the endurance race of parenthood, and extend rations of goodness and patience your family draws upon so hungrily.

Mended People Make Better Parents

Mended mommies and daddies have healthier connections to the wombs from which they came, and to the men and women who did for us what we do now for our own. Feeling connected to a chain of similar souls makes the expectations of intensive parenting seem ridiculously primitive, and a pack of moms and dads coming together to care for their young infinitely sensible. Asking another parent's help becomes second nature, as does asking others to sign a petition so that a fence will be built around a public playground.

Over time, you'll internalize the encouraging words and empathy of fellow child-chasers. Your outlandish reactions to everyday events can be calmed without judgment. And you learn to mother yourself, to believe you deserve as nutritious a lunch as your kids, and to establish a quiet time or a time-out that restores you.

Get Mentored

In the hard times, when you're disappointed in the quality of life afforded you in parenthood or you're about to go postal trying to be the perfect mom, find role models. Look around for mothers who managed to survive the stage you're in and maintained the features of life you hope to maintain: an individual identity, relationships with healthy grown children, a lively marriage, outside interests, and respect from peers. Sometimes more so than in careers and business, mothers need mentors.

A fellow Mount Holyoke alumna, Sybil Stockdale served poached salmon and wisdoms to me on her sunny porch. Mrs. Stockdale, as I feel compelled to call her, endured far more than I can imagine as a new mother whose husband, a navy pilot, was shot down, captured, imprisoned, and tortured for seven years in a North Vietnamese prison camp. (Her husband, Admiral James Stockdale's name will be familiar to you, since he was Ross Perot's vice-presidential running mate in 1992.) During her husband's Vietnam War imprisonment and torture, Mrs. Stockdale quit her teaching job to attend to their four boys; started the first national organization for the families of prisoners of war; allowed top-secret military information to be passed to her husband via her letters; and lobbied silent presidents and leaders to do more to bring home her husband whom she heard from only sporadically. As I shaded four-month-old Liam from the sun and let him suckle the entirety of our conversations, I asked her how she managed all of this.

Mrs. Stockdale experienced periods of profound depression and disorientation during those years and raves about therapists she still can't bring herself to call psychiatrists. Nevertheless, the ever-present needs of her boys, and the other P.O.W. wives, kept her moving when she'd otherwise have succumbed.

Mrs. Stockdale tells me about the first Christmas her husband was a POW, suffering unspeakable brutality at the hands of his guards, and how hard it was for her to prepare for the holidays at home with her children. "Then I realized," Mrs. Stockdale said, "I was in the business of making memories for my boys." From that point on, she tried to treat motherhood as a business, an assembly line of love, affection and values at a time when her children might otherwise have seen the world as a dangerous and horrifying place. (If you get the chance, read the riveting book *In Love and War: The Story of a Family's Ordeal and Sacrifice During the Vietnam Years* Admiral and Mrs. Stockdale wrote together about their experiences.)

Having a paragon like Mrs. Stockdale in my life has been bread and water on my admittedly meager, lousy days. But I collect moments of great motherhood wherever I go. I admire the way one mom I know communicates utter joy and acceptance to her teenagers, letting them know she thinks the teen stage is cool, not intimidating or terrible. I sustain myself some days, thinking about a mom I saw working at a retail store whose baby was stashed under the counter and who kept eyeing the back nervously for the manager. I smile, thinking of my friend's aching back, as she carried her two-year-old daughter—completely overwhelmed and refusing to walk—the entire span of Disneyland for two long days.

Me, a Role Model?

You, too, will be a model for others. A failure of birth control made my friend Dalia's second pregnancy a bittersweet surprise. She was already besieged by motherhood and her lack of enjoyment of it. "Too often I feel like a robot, like my entire life is taken up with routine chores. And sometimes I really despise my kids. They can be very mean. No one ever told me that I might feel this way."

To a few treasured mommy friends, Dalia risked being thought of poorly and admitted she regretted being a mother, especially the second time around. They assured her that alternately adoring and loathing your children, and feeling wildly aggrieved about the amount of work required of you, is *completely normal*. Any women caught off guard by a second pregnancy so quickly after a first, would be distraught and entertain reservations.

In this honest and sanguine way, Dalia's friends became both her support network and models of a less-than-perfect but perfectly-fine form of motherhood. Easing up the standards, and assigning to moms new badges of honor that include emotional breakdowns and everyday meltdowns, Dalia made a home for acceptance, joy, and love amid circumstances she might not have chosen.

Cynthia, a mom who home-schools her two daughters in Alabama, says her greatest peace comes with defying stereotypes, given the absence of African-American role-model mothers in the media. "One rarely hears positive things about being an African-American mother. We hear about single mothers, welfare mothers, crack mothers, overweight mothers, mothers whose children are failing in public school, and mothers on a fast-track to the corporate elite—you know, the black mothers who do it all. Rarely do I hear about plain old, happy African-American mothers."

To become a plain old happy mother, order-in lessons from mothers you hope to model and you'll be nourished by their humanness and determination. Food for the journey, you'll someday be manna for other moms you meet along the way.

Sanctify Yourself

Most days, the volume of my boys' "inside voices" is such that I can't tell if it's Sinatra or Raffi on the stereo. But I think that Simple Minds song "Sanctify Yourself" ought to be an anthem for moms: "Sanctify yourself, set yourself free."

My friend Herb Benson, M.D., a founder and the medical director of Harvard's Mind/Body Medical Institute, believes that the lullabies, poems, and prayers that appeased us as children evoke a special kind of healing in adults. Perhaps this is because we experience rituals in childhood at a formative time in brain development, and this wiring, once recalled, is especially powerful. Or perhaps young people experience mind-body connections naturally, the way adults have to be re-taught to do, once we become conditioned to separate beliefs from physiology, feelings from facts.

In any case, many cancer and other patients who come to Benson and his team for help, elicit a profound physiologic state of relaxation by meditating or focusing their minds, for example, on a Spanish blessing their mother said to them before they left for school or a song they learned in Sunday school. Time and time again in his forty-year medical and research practice, Benson has observed the deep reserves of physical calm and healing that can be summoned by repeating simple traditions from our childhoods.

As a parent, you probably intuitively grasp this—the heaviness of a seemingly light ritual in the everyday life of your family and the way kids latch onto and assign meaning to little traditions you start. Lots of parents mention they love the bedtime customs, from books to songs to tucking-in, and I suspect it is because many of us want to convey the peace we felt as children in the time-honored tradition of the kiss goodnight.

On the fourteenth read of *Harold and the Purple Crayon* in a week, I pretend I'm being recorded for a prestigious readers' series, which rouses me to use inflection and add flourishes. Sometimes, after I've barked at my kids for demanding another song, I end up giving a thirty-minute concert. I get immersed in singing, in the choir music and Broadway tunes that were such a big part of my junior high and high school life.

Mindfulness, Schmindfulness

Lots of experts will tell you that satisfaction in motherhood comes with "being fully present" with your children—advice which frankly never sat well with me or my friends. I suppose they mean this should be our goal—settling into, focusing on, and seeing the beauty in the moment.

So, let me get this straight, you want me to be more *mindful* of the inane and relentless power struggle I have each night with my three-year-old about construction worker pajamas? You're telling me to *get one with* facts I've only grudgingly accepted—that my sleep is interrupted nightly by my children's visits and that "family vacation" is in truth a masochist's dream come true? I would rather go to a third soccer game every Saturday of my already soccer-subjugated life than submit to this advice.

This is probably just semantics. Because Zen masters and mommies-with-attitude aspire to the same thing: greater health and fulfillment. But it's a heck of a lot easier to sell moms on the idea of "infusing routines with passion" or to "lend greater meaning" to a life that feels lackluster. Indeed, the happiest moms I know have learned to temper the stresses of marathon motherhood by sanctifying their experiences, sharing with others the absurd circumstances they find ourselves in, harking back to their pasts, and winnowing from everyday life little moments of transcendence.

Like them, I am bolstered knowing that my mom felt the same way, and that nearly every mother in recorded history has resented a lopsided share of grunt work and the mixed blessings of loving her children and family so deeply. I live for moments when I see in my boys' eyes the same wonder I felt when my mom and dad lit candles on an advent wreath on our dining room table. I've also grown to love country music as a mom because so many of the songs sanctify my experience, paying tribute to ordinary life and personal sacrifices, the struggle of keeping a marriage alive, food on the table, and kids out of trouble.

My friend Elena inherited an incredible oceanview home in a treasured but bohemian part of San Diego. Ocean Beach is chock-full of tattoo and piercing parlors, stoned surfers, and still-faithful Deadheads—not exactly the gingerbread village Elena dreamed of raising her kids in. After all, when she was little, Elena lived in a very homogenous neighborhood in the suburbs with a huge backyard and scads of kids her age to ride bikes with until late on summer nights.

Recently, as an anniversary of her mother's death approached, Elena got keen on selling this incredibly valuable property in Ocean Beach to obtain the utopia she'd had as a child. Then she realized there was no going back. She could not make her mother come back, nor recapture an idyllic world that no longer exists— for any of us who are modern parents.

"That's when I realized how great it is to walk from our house to the beach, the farmer's market, and to get ice cream. My kids are going to be so creative, so energized being this close to the ocean, seeing it through our windows every day." Counting her blessings in the here and now, Elena finally sanctified her family's home.

How can you do get started in this holy business? Figure out what it is you love to do with your kids—baking, exercising, painting, reading, dancing—and make sure you get to do it as much as you can, as sanely as possible. Set aside the preoccupations that do not matter. And with an engaging inflection, a twinkle in your eye, or a professed secret plan, swing a cistern of incense over your daily routines. This is "making memories," the very memories your children will call upon when they become parents.

New moms reported strange primal urges, including:

"A fierce protectiveness, almost like a mother bird protects her nest."

"Burning desire for another baby, out of fear that I'd be left childless if something happened to my first child."

"Fear of flying, fear of skiing, fear of any risk that might leave my son without a mom."

"The inability to hand my child over to a babysitter—something I never expected."

"Tension when the baby cries. The louder he gets, the faster I would drive the car. My heart just races."

"I feel guilty and distracted when I'm away from my six-month-old daughter—even if it's just for an occasional date with my husband or coffee with a friend."

"I never want to have sex, for fear of getting knocked-up again."

"My heart is on my sleeve; I cry at the slightest sentimental provocation."

"I feel as though we need a bigger nest egg, a better house, a more stable life."

Our Expert Tips for
Raising Grandparents

"Establish boundaries as new parents such as 'Call before you come,' or 'We will celebrate Christmas at home.'"

"Let them spoil your kids."

"Limit lengths of visits so you leave them wanting more."

"Accept gifts and advice graciously; dump the undesirables later."

"Urge them to record or write stories/memories for kids to keep."

"Have your kids call them to say hello."

"Tell them about tax benefits they can get from making college savings contributions."

"Factor your parents' health and energy into babysitting or outing plans."

"Don't expect them to change dramatically at their age!"

I Want a Lover, Not a Loafer!

Helping Your Husband Be a Great Father

> SECRET: *Men are slower to transform, but transform they must for marriage and family life to thrive.*

❀ There's no one more entrancing nor sexier than a father absorbed in his children. Ralph Lauren tapped into this feeling a few years ago with magazine ads in which a dad drew his son close while resting in a hammock. That, too, seems to be every new dad's dream—that of enjoying play and leisure time with an energetic and amiable little chap or princess.

Coincidentally, I gave a hammock to Duke on his first Father's Day—an irony, he points out, since the hammock has gathered dust in our garage for all but a few afternoons in seven years of parenthood. As it turns out, fatherhood is not the lazy American pastime the illusory hammock would have it be.

Dads Hold the Keys

Truth be told, a father cradles in his arms the very promise of happy marriage and healthy family life. Research shows that in couples with children, the extent to which a husband and father is engaged in or has been transformed by fatherhood, is the single most important indicator of whether a marriage will last. Dads who tend to munchkins also tend to marriages, deterring parental depression, anxiety, marital conflict, and divorce. Our mates are also the key ingredient in rearing healthy children who adapt and perform well in school.

In their landmark, long-term studies of married-with-children folk, authors of *When Partners Become Parents* Carolyn and Philip Cowan found that men who *actively* parent feel better about themselves, their wives feel more supported, marital conflict is reduced, and their children have fewer behavior problems. Wives of on-duty dads report they have better luck at solving problems in the marriage and feel happier with their unions. And happier couples are less likely to introduce dysfunctional throwbacks from their childhoods into their new families.

In the final trickle-down of this daddy domino effect, a closer relationship between parents, cultivated in part in the Cowans' couples groups, propelled children to significantly higher academic performance, starting in kindergarten and extending into grade school.

Predicting Divorce with One Chat

John Gottman is the University of Washington's marriage guru who can, by observing one conversation between spouses, predict with 95 percent accuracy their potential for divorce. Gottman developed his criteria over years of studying couples in his so-called Love Lab in Seattle, learning that arguments and talks contain unmistakable truths about a marriage that foretell the relationship's triumph or doom.

Gottman is unequivocal in saying that "men must be transformed by parenthood to stay in sync with wives who experience the earlier and more profound metamorphosis into mothers." Indeed, a husband's empathy for his wife, and his ability to tune in to her feelings about the changes motherhood brings, makes a lasting and satisfying marriage far more certain.

"Uh-oh," I hear many of you saying, as I did when I first read these findings, my husband furiously kicking away the demands of parenthood like a chorus line dancer fearing a layoff. The good news is, however, that Cowan and Cowan found that men typically lag a year behind their wives in accepting the mantle of parenthood and adapting to their new roles. Maybe because their early involvement with babies is limited to diaper changes, short outings, and occasional feedings, dads accustom themselves more gradually to parenthood, and to the feeling of having been run over by a bus.

As much as he's now enthralled by his sons, my resident expert, Duke, describes early fatherhood in less than glowing terms: "The first days were euphoric; I held the baby a lot because you were so achy and tired. Then when we got Patrick home, the colic set in, which was devastating. I was good for nothing; Patrick only got more agitated when I held him. You kept telling me the baby could read the tension in my body language, but how could I not be tense when he screamed for hours at a time?"

Duke continues, "I looked forward to going to work because there I had a modicum of control. At home, much of the time I felt unwanted and resented. Of course, when things started going sour at work, I didn't feel particularly comfortable anywhere."

Recalling actor and dad Paul Reiser's joke in his personal account *Babyhood,* Duke said that with the addition of a baby, I went from "entertainment center to juice bar." Duke continues, "I took the drop in sex personally—that you were rejecting me. Eventually I adapted to sex being much more about relaxation than lust, but that's a major adjustment."

Most other forms of entertainment are cut off, too. "You can't watch TV with toddlers around, heck, you can't even sit down. You can't read a book anymore. The yard and my workbench are the only places I can find peace. Even so, I'm too tired most of the time to do anything but take a nap."

And, finally, "It takes a really long time before a child is fun. And if you've only had limited exposure from socializing with friends who have kids, you don't expect a child to be as difficult as they are, or for as long as they are."

The Feelings We Share

Listening to Duke now, I feel for him and the troubles he withstood in the transition. In fact, the more I hear from expectant and new fathers, the more willing I am to admit that many of our circumstances—-as partners becoming parents—are the same. The remarks one expectant dad made in a parenting chat room, hit home: "I thought that expectant fathers were meant to feel joyful, excited, and protective of their partner and unborn baby. [Instead] I'm resentful, scared, and I feel very, very guilty, because my wife has to cope with me expressing negativity whenever we discuss the pregnancy, and although she understands my mixed feelings, it's starting to upset her."

A sympathetic father who replied to the post said, "Where the hell did you get [the delusion of happy expectant dads] from? Most expectant dads, when they first hear, are scared, worried, anxious, etc. One of the big differences is that most keep it to themselves (or post it on here!), and don't tell the missus. It's a credit to your relationship that you can tell her how you feel, although you do need to make room for her feelings. Take some time out to listen to her, and she'll find it easier to do the same for you."

New moms and dads do suffer from many of the same hard feelings, namely grief for their former lives; ineptitude at child care; exhaustion; resentment; and shame for feeling the way they do. In retrospect, I can see that Duke and I could have communed together with these complaints. Instead, we clubbed each other for first place in the misery department.

The *Real* Division of Labor

Empathy fatigue plagues most parents. We play one-upmanship over "who had the worst day" rather than acknowledging "I want attention" signals that underlie the venting match. I'm told dads who are sole breadwinners feel they go out everyday to slay a dragon and drag it home, only to be greeted with contempt, as if they don't contribute to parenthood by providing food and shelter.

New dads often react to having a little dumpling by throwing themselves into their work and worrying about their breadwinning potential, which the Cowans tell us is actually a good sign. Just as a mom "nests," a father feels he must lay in provisions for the nest. While he may need to temper his breadwinning fervor, his fervor nevertheless is a telltale sign that he loves his new baby and has been scooped up by the life-transforming experience of parenthood.

Fathers also want acknowledgment for doing more than their fathers and role models did. Yet, many moms tell me their husbands describe themselves as "babysitters." Or, about times they care for a baby alone, a husband will say, "I'm giving my wife a break," or "I'm letting my wife sleep in this morning." Always is the inference that the baby is the mom's job, and that he is only an occasional substitute. Of course these attitudes are reinforced in airports or Home Depot, where any stroller Dad pushs or any itsy bitsy spider he models is heralded by strangers as extraordinary and adorable.

The bottom line is that mothers still do the lion's share of child and household care in American homes, despite the fact that most of us also work outside the home. And unless moms and dads are very assertive and hyperconscious about the balance of care, stereotypical gender roles return, even if the couple enjoyed an egalitarian marriage before children came along.

Breast-feeding, Night Feedings, and Other Perils

From the very start, breast-feeding can seal the fate of couples who intend to be equal mates. As beneficial as it is for baby and mom, breast-feeding has serious consequences for shared parenting, which experts have yet to address.

To promote breast-feeding, doctors and lactation specialists discourage the use of bottles in the first month of a baby's life. Several pediatricians with whom I consulted said that in the course of their careers, they have never seen a case of "nipple confusion," in which a baby prefers sucking from a bottle rather than the breast. There are many reasons to hold off on supplemental bottles of formula, which babies sometimes prefer over breast milk. But taboos about dads offering bottles of mom's pumped and stored breast milk from an early point seem increasingly baseless.

Yet, feedings are not the only way to establish closeness. Babies do acclimate to dads, or to any caregiver who spends more time with them, scientists tell us. Too often, though, dads get discouraged at not having the magic touch and back off. For this reason, or because moms won't share, dads often get fewer of the exquisite perks babies and children bring: pudgy arms and legs that flail in recognition when you near the crib, the sweet-smelling head that nuzzles under your chin during story time, or the pictures colored at day care they're so excited to give to you.

When Dad withdraws from Baby, this devastating gulf translates to the marriage. Temperamental babies scare dads off even more, and cause a more severe decline in marital satisfaction than relatively contented babies. And while a mom who feels inept will often seek help or direction from others, a male will not, only furthering the family's estrangement.

Several mommy friends of mine reported their husbands were actually better at handling babies than they were. But a larger contingent reported men too impatient to learn baby care, or wired so tightly that they would overreact to spit-up on their shirts or three-year-olds not playing Chutes and Ladders by the rules. New dads everywhere seemed to get huffy about minor annoyances—bubbles blown in milk or toppled Stride Rites spilling playground sand onto hardwood floors.

The arrangements couples made for nighttime feedings also proved prophetic. Some moms prefer to take over at night in order to hand off their screaming gremlins in the evening when dads return from work. But Cowan and Cowan learned that husbands who get up for night-time feedings, if only to change a diaper or bring Baby to Mom, send a critical message of "teamwork" that buffers the marriage against resentment.

What kind of resentment, you ask? Well, when I was a new mom, I handled chow calls two or three times a night between the hours of 11 P.M. and 5 A.M. After putting the little porker down in his crib, I'd shuffle back to bed. At which time my husband would magically rouse himself to murmur, "You're such a good mom."

At his sweet nothings, a burning rage seared through me, so that it was all I could do to fight off the momentary urge to smother him with his fluffy pillow. Fortunately for him, the Sandman wrestled me to the bed and I was asleep before I could plot another step in Duke's down-feathered doom.

Another example? Aimee, a mother of four and a part-time pharmaceutical executive, detailed to my mompool the intellectual feats for which her husband is known. Then after a pause, she blurted out, "But he is *such* a f@*&#*! imbecile. Simple things like getting the kids dressed or fed are beyond him. His lack of compassion is utterly appalling. His answer to everything infant-related was, 'Stick the boob in the baby.'"

Little Gestures Help Sustain Marriage

Perhaps not surprisingly, murderous rage and cursing your husband's name don't contribute to lasting matrimony. Marriage guru Gottman has shown that little gestures of tenderness—kisses, compliments, neck rubs, and kind looks—sustain a marriage over time. Couples who, during an argument can refrain from eye-rolling or disdainful sarcasm and who can extend a love tap or inside joke, demonstrate that their love is here to stay—no matter how loud the accusations get. Indeed, couples who stay together send five times more affectionate signals than hostile ones. Those headed for divorce court average closer to a 1 to 1 ratio.

Of course, libido-less moms avoid kissing or affection for fear they will turn their husbands on. And many women I know feel their eyes are permanently spun skyward, having absorbed many disillusionments and disappointments before and after baby arrived. The inevitable cooling of hot-lava love that occurs a couple years into new marriages now coincides with the disappointing showing dads make in parenthood. This double shot of disillusionment is hard on hormonal moms who already see the glass as half-empty.

Dads and Postpartum Depression

Admittedly, dealing with a postpartum mother's moods is no cakewalk. Listen to this on-line chat-room dad who is worried about his wife: "I think my wife is suffering from postnatal depression. She's always been a very emotional person, prone to losing her temper over the slightest thing. But the six months since our son was born have been the worst ever."

He continues, "I have seen our doctor, who says she can only do something if my wife goes to see her. My wife refuses to admit there's a problem, blaming me for being unsupportive and selfish. I admit I'm probably not the greatest husband/father in the world, but I do know I've been as helpful and involved as I can be and do my best to take the baby so she can have time to herself."

However, the "imbecile" to whom Aimee is married was far less compassionate. She explains, "I had horrible postpartum depression. Once I was sitting on the stairs, crying and telling him I felt as if I was going to kill myself. Then the baby started crying and instead of taking charge, he handed me the baby! It's as if there is no connection between my suffering and his actions. How can he see me suffer and not intervene?"

Men often feel particularly blindsided by the hormonal repercussions of childbirth and new parenthood. If doctor's office visits and prenatal classes fail to inform us of the potential for emotional upheaval, imagine how shell-shocked our husbands feel.

They also have their own life crises to attend to. Becoming a father often prompts a man's coming of age, and a reassessment of his priorities and professional aspirations. This passage makes men feel middle-aged, as they pull out from sports or outings with the guys that kept them feeling young.

Better Marriages, As Time Goes By?

For fathers and marriages that are struggling, problems don't necessarily resolve over time. Babies become toddlers who test limits, and out-of-sync mates often disagree on how to handle discipline or inappropriate behavior. Researchers tell us arguments over parenting styles hit moms hard, contributing to an even more desperate unhappiness in the marriage.

At this juncture, women, who tend to be the more skilled relationship-builders, have zero motivation to tend to a spouse's ailing ego or an increasingly disappointing marriage. We assume a grown man can take care of himself, and that a marriage can fly on auto-pilot for awhile. One mom I know admits she's become considerably less compassionate toward her husband. "If he has a pain or a headache, to me it seems way overboard. I want to yell at him, 'Toughen up!' Whereas with my child, I'd do whatever he needed."

Little children, with their freckled noses and butter-soft skin, are downright captivating. It's far easier to devote one's time to a toddler who's eager to learn, in contrast to a spouse who never seems to learn.

When Happy Marriages Sour in Parenthood

Katrina, an Ohio mother of a four-year-old girl, is in the midst of a divorce and realizes in hindsight how parenthood starved her marriage. "I felt we had a great relationship before parenthood. I don't want to say that having a baby caused the divorce, but many of our problems of decreased physical intimacy and feelings of neglect started during pregnancy."

While babies don't cause divorces, the stresses that new parents face are often insurmountable for couples who can't tone down their antagonism or devote time to one another. Let's hope your relationship is one of the fourth of all marriages that sails through early parenthood contentedly. But if you've experienced the undertow that enormous stress often brings, acknowledge that there's danger in your husband's distance and follow the advice below.

Draw Him in, and Set Him up to Succeed

Right this moment, think about how you could make parenting a less daunting prospect for a husband who has sidelined himself. If you or your snazzy dressed toddler laid out clothes the night before, Dad could more easily tackle the morning routine. If you ordered pizza and TiVo'ed a family movie before your mommy's night out, wouldn't Dad be nudged into meeting your expectations and taking better care of the kids while you're gone?

Two months after Liam was born, Duke and I took the family to Las Vegas for a two-day stay at Circus, Circus Hotel. The five-hour drive we'd timed carefully to naps and *The Land Before Time* videos turned into eight teeth-clenching, baby-crying hours on a freeway under construction, with cars all around us overheating in the 119-degree heat. We barreled into town just in time for a show at the Excalibur Hotel, a medieval meal, and a tournament of knights over which three-year-old Patrick had been salivating for weeks. Only we got lost on several one-way avenues, which sent Duke's blood pressure soaring.

Duke resorted to yelling and cursing. He blamed this wretched trip on me, blasted the detailed planning I'd done, and mocked my good sense with words I'm so glad I don't remember. This argument marked the culmination of so many disappointing smaller trips in the past year—excursions to parks or zoos in which Patrick, the baby, or I did something that sent Duke over the edge, his bad humor always a thin layer of tolerance away from exploding.

I hollered back, and the trip passed uneventfully, the baby sleeping relatively well and Patrick wowed by the lights at night on the strip and the idea of a McDonald's being right downstairs in our hotel. But the eroding respect my husband showed me, and the dread I was developing of his temper, made this argument very different for me than the rest.

Duke did stop yelling at me then. For two more years, he shouted, overreacted, and insulted the kids, spanking more than the limited amount we agreed we would. Each time he yelled, I believed a little piece of my children's souls died. So I did what a girl schooled on "killing them with kindness" does: I tried even harder to manage everyone's behavior, and bypass any hiccup or flare-up with my own burst of energy, humor, or distraction. Time and again, however, Duke's eruptions stole from me precious memories that I could never recapture, as one then the other of our kids lost his baby fat and took on the stance of a boy.

More than anything else, this was the reason I got into my minivan one day, collapsed into hysterical tears, and feared that fleeing was imminent. Duke never intended to hurt us, I was sure, but his upbringing and his constitution had not prepared him for the hands-on, tender loving parenting I expected and that I believed the boys deserved.

No matter how many times I tried to impress upon him that our energy-siphoning boys were not overactive delinquents, no matter how many times we talked about his being the most important gender model in their lives, the tirades returned. And my loving arms got too tired to continue shielding the boys from their dad's faults, and their dad from the boys' mishaps.

Making the Turn

At this endpoint, in which I realized my mental and emotional health were at risk, I offered Duke some alternatives: an anger management course, a parenting course we'd take together, or long-term therapy. Thank goodness, he took me up on the first two and began examining and untangling the snarls of married-with-children life he'd previously blamed on everyone else.

To bolster him in this vulnerable time, I set him up to succeed. I suggested he build a tree house, which would give him an outlet for stress and make him a hero in our boys' eyes. I designed smaller outings matched to his energy and blood sugar levels, and offered an extra set of hands in a non-threatening way when he began to lose his cool. I encouraged him to bow out sometimes if he couldn't muster the energy and to apologize to Patrick and Liam after a blow-up. And I stopped challenging his authority in front of the

kids, semi-regularly putting a sock in my mouth to prevent critiques of his performance.

It's astonishing to see the effects of Duke's decision to learn to
be a better dad, and of my invitation to him to be involved in family life in ways he was sure to triumph. The guys love to brag to
their friends that Dad built the tree house, complete with two stories, a pirate's scope, tire swing, water slide, and climbing wall. And
a psychiatrist told me the boys were almost better off with a dad
who apologized for losing his temper than with an even-tempered
dad. "He's modeling for them that we all make mistakes, and that
acquiring new skills is possible."

It felt like a death when I gave up on Duke parenting equally, and
accepted that, as the parent with greater skills, I was called to do
more. I put aside enormous anger at having to do prep work to enhance the relationships for which my husband was responsible. Yet,
what I wanted more than to flee was a fulfilling, healthy family life.
Not a divorce. Not a back alley where I could swear drunkenly under my breath about a stalled revolution. So, while Duke improved
his parenting dexterity, I devised ways to bring him gracefully into
our circle, and make him feel at home in his own home.

The investment I've made, and the bigger person I've forced
myself to become, has paid off grandly. The relationships Patrick
and Liam now enjoy with their dad, and the times they reach for
him instead of me, are evidence of how incredibly far we've come,
the ethos of respect and unconditional love now thick in our interactions.

My sons show every sign of sprouting tall and stubborn like
their dad. But when they leave home for some terrific future, they
will know how much they are cherished, albeit by parents who are
always in search of their better selves.

Believe in Babysitters

Before we had kids, dinner guests shared their babysitting morays with us: Except for a handful of evenings when relatives visited, the couple didn't go out by themselves for the first three years of their children's lives—a whopping six years. This mom and dad also didn't allow their half-time nanny to take the kids anywhere in the car. "We would never be able to live with ourselves if an accident were to occur," the mom said.

The "We couldn't live with ourselves if . . ." argument makes me nuts. It's also foolhardy considering how many moms tell me that in retrospect they would have been happier, healthier, and more patient moms had they hired babysitters more often. "I was so afraid," says one veteran mom I know. "But now I realize the kids would have been fine."

Like most moms, I daily contemplate the horror of something happening to one of my precious boys, and am jolted by the nausea-inspiring realization of how vulnerable small children are in a sometimes sick and terrifying world. Yet, we couldn't live with *ourselves*, Duke and I decided, if our marriage floundered from lack of attention, or if cabin fever made us hostile toward our kids. We bought an inexpensive older model Volvo station wagon for our nanny to drive because we worried she could not afford a car with airbags and safety features we'd prefer. Armed with library cards and season passes to the San Diego Zoo, the Scripps Aquarium, Sea World, and a host of Balboa Park museums, our kids and nanny are never at a loss for something interesting to do.

Teenage babysitters fall within my comfort zone because church and neighbor kids, daughters and sons of my parents' friends always babysat for my sister and me. Several of those sitters are friends and role models we correspond with even today. Although this is a different age and time, responsible and smart teenagers are still in plentiful supply and we have the advantage of cell phones our night-on-the-town parents never had.

Babysitting Options

Even if you can't bring yourself to trust a teenager, don't let months and years go by without setting up a swap system with friends, or investigating a cooperative at your church or community center. There is simply nothing healthier you can do for your marriage, with the exception of regular and reciprocal orgasms, than getting out once a week or at least once a month with the love of your life—ahem, that would be your husband, not your baby.

It's understandable for moms who work full-time to feel guilty leaving their little charges with a babysitter on weekends. So curtail your nights out but plan romantic adventures at home. Have a candlelight picnic in your bedroom. Or, pour the wine, light a fire in an outside fireplace, and whisper sweet nothings—with the baby intercom nearby.

Don't be cavalier about choosing babysitters but don't overplay the risks either. Neglected marriages and pleasure-starved mommies and daddies are big risks in themselves.

Apply Your Mother-Sculpted Heart to Your Marriage.

None of us wants to mother our husbands. However, shouldn't our spouses benefit and not be deprived of a heart so dramatically expanded and instructed by motherhood? Marriage is, after all, the second chance many men and women have at healing the wounds of their original families.

Borrowing relationship wisdom from motherhood

What are the key lessons raising a child teaches you that might also shore up a sagging marriage?

- Attachment is fundamental to our well-being and we have to devote time to nurturing it.

- Little things matter . . . a lot.

- There's no reasoning with someone—child or man—who's exhausted or overwhelmed. And tantrums are sure signs a person needs comfort, attention, or rest.

- Love is not always reciprocal.

- Defiance is a natural part of human development, often a reaction to feeling attached and yet needing to distinguish one's self.

- A kiss can heal an ouchie.

- It's very tiring being a good person all day in the outside world and home is a safe place to disintegrate.

If you believe that children are diplomats sent from above meant to reacquaint us with the honest and innocent sides of ourselves, you'll have no trouble incorporating the idea that children are the best marriage counselors. And like mothers themselves, love is screwed up and insane sometimes. Yet, love gets up the next day and tries again, this time apologetic and calmer, happy to have a clean slate upon which to write its poems and knock-knock jokes, its romantic notions and silly human tricks.

Here's Exhibit A: Several months ago, I was running the gauntlet of nighttime compulsories—boiling water for spaghetti, running tepid water for baths, wiping bottoms, correcting homework, fielding

Jedi questions, and hunting down clean pajamas—when I snapped. I left Duke, who needed down-time after work to compose himself for an evening with our Beastie Boys, in charge of one item: taking pasta from a container and dropping it into a pot of water.

When I returned, however, the water on the stove had still not boiled, and I had no pasta to serve my famished boys. I jumped to conclusions, shouting at Duke, "Why did you turn the heat down?!" When he looked at me blankly, I began ranting in a nasal tone, *"I SAW you! I saw YOU! I SAAAAAAAAW YOOOOOUUUU!"* Duke turned on his heel and fled our castle for a walk to Starbucks, leaving his two sons behind to gape at me and my sullied honor.

"Mom," Patrick said, his slippers padding softly on the kitchen province, "Why didn't you just say to Dad that 'I *thought* I saw you turn down the heat under the pot?' Then everything would have been okay."

Shortly thereafter, we got a new stove with a fast-acting burner for pasta. And Duke, Patrick, Liam, and I developed a kind of running joke, a cackle of "I *SAW* you!" to which we resort when one of us needs to lighten up, crack up, or feel the abiding pleasure of a forgiving family.

There are lots of Exhibit Bs I could reveal to you, in which my husband was the bigger culprit. But in my family, an interaction mom bungled, and the willingness mom has to laugh at herself, has been transformative. Maybe that's because moms are really good at teaching love and forgiveness. Maybe that's because often, moms have to teach dads the gifts of relationships dads haven't learned before.

In your worst marriage moments, look for the goodness in this man you think should know better, the same way you do when your toddler colors on the walls. Empathy breeds empathy. In the face of an accepting, indefatigable love, boys do grow up to be men.

Fathers who didn't know how to, find greater reserves of patience and stamina. Or moms discover ways to love them just the same, either by letting go of prescribed expectations or by allowing themselves to be surprised by other forms of goodness.

Stressed-out new moms went for the jugular with their husbands, saying . . .

"He obviously takes after your side of the family in the common sense department."

—Amelia, San Francisco, after their baby son climbed on the stove.

"Be the parent!!!!!"

—Delaney, Washington D.C., when her three-year-old and forty-nine-year-old were fighting.

"I love you but I'm not in love with you anymore."

—Julia, Madison, Wisconsin

"You're such a pansy!"

—Twana, Dallas, to her manly man.

"When I get breast cancer from trying to keep up with everything around here, we'll know who to blame."

—Marilyn, Detroit, Michigan

"You've become your mother."

—Marie, Providence, Rhode Island, lobbing the "ultimate insult."

"Whack off in the shower! Hire a prostitute! Just leave me alone!"

—Patty, New York, feeling less than amorous.

"The baby isn't yours!"

—Ellie, Williamstown, Massachusetts, fabricated in an argument before her divorce.

chapter nine

The Curse of Greatness

Staying Sane Amid the Relentless Demands of Motherhood

> **SECRET:** *Women do more because we are extraordinarily talented, patient, and energetic. Demand the help of husbands, and let the rest go.*

Tell me if this sounds familiar:

Married couple Judy and Tim decided to start a family a few years ago. Judy got pregnant and gave birth to their daughter; Tim was one happy dad.

When the baby was born, Tim took two weeks off from work. Judy's career was sidelined for three years.

For the first year, Judy breast-fed their newborn between six and twelve times a day, and fixed dinner for the family each night. Tim made himself breakfast and an occasional sandwich for the two of them.

Judy educated herself thoroughly about optimal child care and development. Tim shoved "must see" articles Judy cut out into his dresser drawer and forgot about them.

Judy got up two and three times a night to feed or comfort their daughter, enduring the babe's relentless crying and the sleep deprivation it caused. Tim stayed in bed because he had to go to work the next day, while Judy would stay home and continue the child care routine.

Tim worked fifty to sixty hours per week; Judy was on twenty-four-hour call and was responsible for child care, errands, cooking, shopping, cleaning, laundry, bill-paying, buying gifts, making arrangements for baby-sitting, household repairs, medical appointments, social, birthday, holiday and vacation plans.

When Tim wanted to take a shower or run to the hardware store, he did. When Judy wanted to take a shower or work in the garden, she had to ask Tim if he could watch the baby.

When her daughter was sick or Tim went out of town, Judy braced herself for the crises and got through it. When Judy left town, friends called Tim to offer play dates and homemade dinners.

With their daughter, Judy was kind, patient, and attentive, making sure the girl ate right, had quality interactions with Mom, and got enough sleep. When Tim was in charge, their daughter either didn't eat or ate junk, watched TV for hours, and stayed up late.

As much as she loved her little girl, Judy felt overburdened by and resentful of motherhood, but powerless to change established routines or request solutions that might cost more money. Tim was frustrated because Judy didn't appreciate how hard he was working to keep the family afloat. He also felt neglected because Judy wasn't interested in their romantic life anymore.

Needing an Eight-Day Workweek

Slap some cardboard onto the scene above, cut out Judy's face, and nearly every mother I know could pop in and blend in to this scenario. In fact, only 20 percent of marriages feature husbands and wives who share housework fifty-fifty. Even if Judy worked outside the home, as 75 percent of moms do, the division of labor would not be very different. Women who work outside the home on average contribute fifteen hours more than their mates do on child care and household responsibilities, according to the landmark book on the subject, *The Second Shift* by Arlie Russell Hochschild.

So that's what all those "give-him-a-little-break" favors amount to: the hour you get up with the kids before your husband rises; the hours you spend crossing tasks off a mental to-do list while he watches TV or surfs the Net; the baths, books, games, errands, or meal preparations from which he dismisses himself; and the hour or two you stay up when he's already asleep. Indeed, the typical mom needs an eight-day workweek because she spends the equivalent of an entire day's waking hours contributing to her family's cause—namely their everyday upkeep, nourishment, and well-being.

Of all the secrets veteran moms wanted to divulge to new moms, no topic inspired more passion than the uneven division of labor among couples. "All mothers are single mothers" has become the sarcastic motto of aggrieved, wedded moms, who exhaust themselves to crank out full and relatively happy lives. Single moms, of course, would relish the occasional break even a lethargic father could provide, not to mention a second salary. Still, overwrought married moms often believe they would be better off handling everything alone, than expecting more of, and constantly being disappointed by, husbands who don't do their share.

Mel is a new mom from San Francisco who expected her feminist husband would do his part, even though she no longer works outside of the home. "One night my husband, Mike, did the midnight feeding," she explains. "The next day he kept complaining about how incredibly tired he was, and how he had to have a nap. Night after night, I've been doing this, without *ever* getting a nap.

And he acted as if I should be plumping his pillow for getting less than eight hours of sleep one single, solitary night."

Mel continues, "Once, I told Mike about the intense anxiety I feel being a mom. His answer was that he'd stay home and I could go out and *get a job*. His perception is that my staying home with the baby *wasn't* a job. And I can tell you *this* job makes the other jobs I've done look like cake."

Half-Assed Help

As Mel uttered exasperatedly, fathers can bring "attitude" to a domestic or parenting task, as if helping out is a favor or an imposition. Their contribution is often half-assed or halfhearted, moms told me. Expect your child to be dressed in three shades of green if Daddy dressed him. Always inspect the clean-up job Dad does after dinner because a gallon of milk or a pan of leftovers will undoubtedly be left out on a counter to spoil. No joke, it often feels as though you have another child when you have to run interference for a parent whose performance is slipshod or self-absorbed.

Yes, in most cases, our husbands are more engaged in child care than our fathers were. Although their contribution in other household work is not nearly as impressive, dads now care for one in four preschool children for varying periods of time while moms work. As babies become toddlers, then preschoolers and grade-schoolers, our partners, in most cases, do relate better to our children. And, with 25 percent of moms staying at home with young children, many are single breadwinners who enable their wives to have choices—choices to take breaks from the 9 to 5 routine that guys usually don't have.

It's still true that wives can more easily carry the larger load in marriage and family life if husbands appreciate their wives' contribution. The problem is, appreciation does not go far enough nowadays. Moms are getting depleted at a faster rate because the pace of family life and career has never been faster.

Help for Hire

More and more families turn to paid help—cleaning people and lawn services, babysitters, personal chefs, drivers, gophers, and tutors—to bridge the gap. Only one of the tricky messages this sends our kids is that we've given up on equal rights and on men taking more responsibility. We produce another generation of girls and boys predestined to experience back-firing and unfair marriages.

In an *Atlantic Monthly* article that sparked considerable debate, writer/mother Caitlin Flanagan says that because so much of the help on which parents rely today is performed inexpensively by immigrants, we exploit the poor in order to liberate ourselves from the demands of parenthood. She's right. I worry a lot about the class differences elucidated in our home, and about the reluctance of our young boys to clean up after themselves, given that the main figures they see cleaning in our household are a Latina nanny and a Latina cleaning woman. Nevertheless our family's need for dual incomes and Duke's and my desire to pursue simultaneous professional lives are utterly dependent on people who can help us at a price we can afford.

Depleted Mom Syndrome

Missing from Flanagan's article was the hopelessness many moms feel trying to solve this intractable problem alone. Indeed, moms with full-time careers added onto their full-time jobs at home teeter constantly on the edge of burnout, a trend that led authors Rick and Jan Hanson to explore and coin the term *the depleted mom syndrome,* in their book *Mother Nurture.* According to the Hansons, depleted moms feel tired all the time, are susceptible to illness, experience back pains and headaches, emotional numbing, depression, mood swings, irritability, hopelessness, confusion, running battles with husbands, and a turning inward away from friends and family.

"Wow, that's a syndrome?" I hear many of you remarking. "I thought that was just motherhood!" Unfortunately, most of us have come to equate these symptoms with motherhood itself, instead of recognizing the influence of multiple stresses that mount over time. Stress-inducing culprits include: lack of sleep and exercise, poor diet, hormonal imbalances, nutrient loss, neurotransmitter deficiencies, guilt, anxiety, conflicting role expectations, marital conflict, and a breakdown of social supports.

Moms often cope with the syndrome by becoming over-controlling, using children as confidantes or surrogate mates, criticizing others bitterly or exaggeratedly, taking a victim or martyr stance, and/or escaping into distractions and consolations such as overeating or alcohol. Of course, these cures often end up spiraling us right back into despair and exhaustion.

Few moms appreciate that exhaustion and depletion are at the root of their lethargy. A former lingerie designer who now stays home with her long-eyelashed daughter, Sharon describes "being stuck" and unable to tackle work-related tasks that were no-brainers to her in pre-parenthood days. "I've never done well with pauses between projects. But this is ridiculous. I can't seem to get going." This was a common refrain among moms combining consulting work with stay-at-home parenting: switching gears is difficult and paid work is often put off or given the short shift.

Dana, a mom who acknowledges she needs to hire part-time

help for her one- and three-year-old boys, also feels stuck. "It's only a matter of taking an initiative and picking up the phone. But to me, it feels as if I'm crawling out of a tar pit."

The men in our lives often expect us to "snap out of" this pesky syndrome. Trouble is, this syndrome builds up over time and cannot be eliminated with a genie's nod. Moms often suffer so long with this condition that we develop the emotional equivalent to hypothermia, the inability to generate heat on our own. This is depression, the state in which your body stops being able to produce happiness and creative solutions, and you need outside help such as counseling, medication, cognitive therapy, meditation, massage, or other treatments to kick-start your physiology and help restore a balance within.

As I mentioned, when my boys were two and five years old, I got into my minivan one morning to go to my *other* full-time job and dared not turn the key for fear I would keep driving and never come home. Instead of making a run for it, I sat in front of my house, crying into the steering wheel until Duke caught sight of me as he was leaving for work. I told Duke I wanted a doctor to admit me to a hospital, the way celebrities' doctors do.

I slept for four days, rarely leaving my bedroom because the sight of mail sitting unopened on the hall table overwhelmed me. A game piece underfoot would have been my undoing.

My sister called hourly, and friends came over to hold my hand. My therapist called to discuss my dosage of medication, and my boss called and kindly checked on me. Meanwhile Duke sheltered the boys from Mommy's tears.

The toll from ceaseless motion day and night, from being the shock absorber between a tense husband/father and our rambunctious boys, and from manic attention to the mundane—the elastic in socks, the banana consumption of the household—had come due.

Eventually I emerged from the emotional and physical fatigue and sorrow into which I had sunk that morning. I caught sight of blue sky and of the pink hands of little people who loved me. I realized, for the first time, I had a responsibility to take care of the woman on whom my children almost totally relied for their health and growth. I had to find a different way to parent, and my new method had to include mothering myself.

Three Steps for Sanity

How do moms prevent becoming this depleted? How do we demand help from our spouses or accept the injustice that things are not going to change? How do we acknowledge the rage we feel without torching our marriages? Here are some of the conclusions that been-there-done-that moms have come to—bread crumbs for your first visit to this perilous forest.

Hurl Pots, and Then Make a Plan

When my sister and I, thirteen months apart, were both under the age of three, my mom took us to see the pediatrician, concerned about our wakefulness during the night and fussiness during the day. She told the kind doctor how frustrated and worried she was that something was amiss with our behavior.

The pediatrician prescribed two very sound treatment options: "First, install a gate outside of the girls' bedroom so they can't automatically bother you when they wake up. Secondly, go out to your garage once a week while the kids are asleep. Take the extra clay flowerpots you have around and one by one, hurl and smash the pots on the wall."

Hurl pots. *That's* what no one tells a new mom. Rage simply isn't among the traits we expect of cookie-baking, hand-holding mothers. Yet when asked, moms of every age admitted that rage was a defining characteristic of early motherhood.

"One of the worst discoveries of being a parent for me," writes author Anne Lamott, "is the self-discovery, being face to face with one's secret insanity and brokenness and rage . . . that way down deep, way past being kind and religious and trying to take care of everyone, I was seething. Now it's close to the surface. I feel it race from my center up into my arms and down into my hands and it scares the shit out of me."

Rage Virgins

A significant number of moms are rage virgins, having never before encountered major and lasting anger. That this rage comes at a time when they expect and deserve to be happy is especially damning. So what is a new mom, who handles anger as awkwardly as she does a wet, naked, squirming newborn, to do?

Julia, a New York City mother of two, offers, "Resentment builds when you clean urine out of the rug during a potty-training session, when you get 'more milk' for the fifth time during dinner, when you give the same answer to the same question for the umpteenth time, and keep your childs' lives mentally filed with color-coded precision. To keep that anger at bay, I imagine myself being the one thanked first or most effusively when my daughter wins an Academy Award or my son wins *Time*'s Person of the Year. Sometimes this is just what I need to keep from taking my husband's head off."

Time-Outs for Mom

If the tempest erupts in the presence of your child, take a time out. In moments of fury, every parent realizes how capable he or she is becoming violent with a child. Be the best role model you can and show little fireball Devon how to count to ten, take deep breaths, or leave a situation till you can calm down.

If you're seething over your rights being trampled, try not to hiss and spew indiscriminately at your spouse. Ultimately, the paintball game in which you shoot splats of anger at him will only make him defend himself or run off. You won't change him and his loafing ways, unless you have a more strategic plan.

Start taking your livid self out of the house on a regular basis for cool-downs. This in itself will be progress, a decision to put yourself first, say, one night each week. Split a three-hour break in half, one part for pampering or exercise, one part for hard thinking. (If you decide to exercise, work out long or hard enough for endorphins to kick in. That sweet rush of adrenaline is darn near orgasmic for tight-wired moms.)

When you've de-stressed a bit, take some time to consider these valuable lessons from psychologist and author Harriet Lerner, Ph.D., in her book *The Dance of Anger: A Woman's Guide to Changing the Patterns of Intimate Relationships*:

- Venting anger may not help. It tends to protect or solidify, rather than challenge, the existing rules or patterns of a relationship.

- The only person we can truly change or control is our own self.

- Blaming and fighting are often ineffective methods for exacting change, and ways to avoid the more threatening job of changing your self.

Before you close this book in disgust, furious that I would add one more straw of responsibility to your bedraggled camel's back, know this: The frustrated sighs, the sarcastic comments, and the new low to which you stoop in arguments with your partner will doom your relationship. Unless you truly want to be single again, you must approach the giant phallic symbol of injustice in your living room in a less vindictive way.

My friends and I know you would rather crawl across broken glass on your hands and knees. But trust us, if you change your attitude and expectations first, often though not always, your husband may surprise you by changing, too.

Change Course

In the sleep-deprived haze of baby care, most couples settle for the easiest solution—Mom's breast and comfort—instead of ensuring that the baby associates Dad with comfort, too. Unless early on you started leaving Chloe with Dad for several hours at a time, neither duckling nor man with ruffled feathers will now be comfortable in a pond without you. In this way, the combo of child dependence and underdeveloped Dad is often the death knell of equal parenting.

Despite how well babyhood trained you, couples can renegotiate and share more responsibilities. Truth is most husbands and fathers are willing to help more but they simply do not know how to carve a role out for themselves. From lack of either nature or nurture, guys don't look at an empty table and perceive it the way women do: that the table needs placemats, napkins, silverware, and glassware for a meal. Nor do they look at a baby's snot-covered face and immediately conjure, "I should get a tissue!" Men's brains don't work that way, and women are cursed with a mind for detail, so experts tell us that wives often have to detail to their mates what needs doing.

Tell Him What You Need Him to Do

You don't have to nag. Just state what you need. All these months, perhaps even years, you thought your spouse was a slug or a jerk, either neglecting or assuming you would set the table or wipe the nose. When cognitively, he really did need you to say, in the same firm but positive voice you'd use to teach your kids: "Honey, please set the table with placemats, napkins, silverware, and cups." Or, "Sweetheart, please get a tissue and wipe the baby's schnozz."

Again the way you would with a three-year-old, remark afterward, "Great job setting the table!" or "Don't you feel good, having met your baby's need for mucous relief?" You're seething that he hasn't lifted a finger for years, but if you want him to start, you have to coddle him.

Reward Him Royally

Which brings us to sexual favors . . . the male species is highly suggestible if you reward them in the single-minded way they single-mindedly adore. I bought my husband's vote for Al Gore in the 2000 presidential election by offering up a treat he only otherwise gets on birthdays. If I made that sacrifice for a political party, only to be thwarted by a handful of Florida votes and hanging chads, you can make it occasionally for the sake of your sanity, too.

Tag Teams and Other Methods

Other tried-and-true methods my mommy friends recommend? Prioritize your most pressing household needs and then divvy up duties based on jobs you can stomach, and those that he can bear. Trade off, do together, or hire help for the items neither of you cares to do.

In child care, adopt a tag-team approach, in which he gets to play golf on Saturday mornings if you get Sunday evening for a movie with friends. If you have a couple little darlings, split errands so that each parent has only to tend to one child.

Enlist Your Tike

As early as appropriate, get your child involved with chores or meal preparation. Busy moms often forget to delegate as their charges grow and become more capable. Yet, two-year-olds get a kick out of wiping countertops and spritzing plants, and three-year-olds can be champion wastebasket-emptiers and clean diaper–fetchers. Of course, research demonstrates that kids help out more in families in which fathers chip in on household chores—so there's more grist for the man-helping mill.

Renegotiate with the Help of a Therapist

The floor dropped out from under a friend of mine three years into parenthood. It was the middle of the night, one of several in a series in which Carole Ann had to awaken to strip her daughter's soaked sheets and remake the bed. Carole Ann's husband stayed in bed, rationalizing that he had never felt the rush his wife did to get their toddler out of diapers. "The full weight of my anger and re-sentment hit that night," Carole Ann remembers. "The marriage I had expected to be a partnership was a farce."

As a result, potty training was put off in favor of marriage ther-apy. And today, with three daughters and a swing set that keeps the kids occupied while Mom and Dad sneak away for a "quickie" in the bathroom, Carole Ann's marriage is all grown-up and contented again.

Nearly half of the couples I talked to for this book have taken their turn on a counselor's couch, and many of them credit it with saving their marriage from the anger that threatened to consume it.

As one mom told me, "Our counselor helped us listen to each other and appreciate that both of us felt aggrieved. She urged us not to resort to fifty-fifty thinking but to acknowledge that both of us were giving 80 percent. With the stresses of early parenthood, way too much was being asked of both of us."

Desperate Measures

Desperate measures may be needed if your husband won't pitch in, won't agree to counseling, and wonders what the big deal is about all the work you do. For several weeks, keep track of the hours you're spending on all your responsibilities. The same way you'd show a detailed project report to an untrusting boss, sometimes you can clarify for the nitwit what a job entails. Or why you need, ahem, more staffing to get the job done.

Depending on how desperate you are, those of you working without income might consider getting a part-time job or going back to work sooner than you originally planned. Also, if you've been doing paid work from home albeit with child care, you may benefit from dressing up and leaving for work—even if you're going to a coffee shop with your laptop. It's blasphemous, I know, but husbands help more when you're officially suited up and leaving the hearth for work. God knows where they got the idea that you're lounging around and eating bonbons, but sometimes it's not worth trying to dissuade them of their delusions. Get a regular paycheck, and concessions may emerge.

Hubbies with Puffed-Up Professions

Many of you are undoubtedly up against men who think their jobs are gonzo-important—far more essential to the Western world than yours. If our hubbies were chief negotiators in the Middle East Peace talks, Mars explorers, or producers of the *Oprah* show, we might understand why they couldn't possibly take Jimmy to his doctor's appointment, or pick up Kentucky Fried Chicken on their way home. Until lots of ladies complained about this, I thought this was a symptom of military life—that Duke considered his job requirements inviolate while mine were negligible. But even husbands who bring home less moolah than their wives, or hold down lower profile jobs, often insist their schedules take precedence.

In which case, you may occasionally need to leave your mate hanging. Not your child, because none of us can stand the thought of that. Let's say on Saturday you leave for a bridal shower, and then take up a friend's invitation for dinner afterwards. Don't call to tell him you're going to be later than you planned. Call him to tell him you're at dinner and that you'll be home when you and your friend have a chance to catch up. That's what he does when he calls after work and says he's stopping for an officemate's farewell party, without thinking about the roustabouts you've had to restrain from pulling the stuffing out of the couch for the last three hours.

He's the Martyr, But You're the Hero

Brace yourself after time away for martyrdom tales—meant to induce guilt—and for the less-than-savory appearance of your beloved children and home. Allow yourself to have empathy fatigue; let the sandman take away minor irritants he experienced rather than internalizing it yourself.

Finally, recognize that the goose who leads beautiful, arrowhead-shaped flight formations south, does almost all the work for the entire flock. She takes the impact, slicing the wind with her wings, while the others catch her air. That's what mothers do. We're the Michael Jordans of family life, leading our teams because we're born leaders, working harder because most of the time, we have more stamina or do things more efficiently.

If you have a more nurturing temperament or more patience for teaching complicated steps, you're going to be better off helping your first-grader with homework, or volunteering at the school. Good marriages are made up of people with different and complementary abilities, not necessarily abilities that can be applied equally.

Cultivate a Secret Life

To consistently perform to your ability, however, you must take care of yourself. And that's where most moms falter, because *In-Style* magazine does not interview a movie-star's nanny nor tell us about the manicure appointments the celeb goes to instead of taking "baby and me" classes at Gymboree.

The same way doctors cover up for celebrity patients, I had to learn to cover up for myself. Based on what society expected of me in what it deemed my most important role in life, I persuaded myself it was shameful to resent motherhood, shameful to want more from life than my beautiful husband and children. In my rush to provide for others the past five years, I denied myself personal pleasures: trips to the library in which *I* got to choose a book; massages and leisurely museum strolls; walks alone, and window-shopping; writing in my journal in a café, or sitting on a beach by myself.

Yet, I could not imagine embracing a life that openly allowed me these treats, when my kids spent half their weekdays with a caretaker. So I created my "secret life"—tunnels and hideaways into which my soul could duck and cover for a furtive half-hour, three hours, or an entire weekend. I didn't ask permission to spend money or take the time. I didn't tell anyone where I'd been or what I'd done. I just went somewhere my heart desired, took in something that I would appreciate more than anyone, and stashed the pleasure away like a ring from a boyfriend who comes from the wrong side of the tracks. In secret I can feel the weight and giggly expanse of it, the fullest measure of pleasure, without worrying what anyone else will think.

It's really sad that moms feel they must go underground to care for themselves. It's unconscionable that our society should expect us to march our progeny into good citizenship, without regard for our own health and sustenance. But most moms I know don't have the wherewithal to defend their needs at the same time they're working full-time, getting kids to school, supporting their husbands' careers, caring for aging parents, providing snacks for sports and extracurricular activities, volunteering, and fund-raising for their children's schools or organizations.

So we have to have top-quality chocolate stashed somewhere only we know about. A book of sonnets in the bathroom. A massage therapist or make-up counter on speed dial. Or, a list of "favorite places I never get to go" folded and pressed into the glove compartment.

Believe me, you never want to go to the well and hear the bucket scraping rock on the bottom. You never want to feel, as I did once, that you and your family are hanging by this rope, coming up plaited with despair and dry as a bone. You have to find a way to keep your spirit moist and alive, both for yourself and for the sake of your family.

Adopt a "Whatever Works" Mentality

A mother of three once told me how she handled it when her children's pacifiers fell on the floor: "With the first baby, I washed and sterilized it. With the second, I wiped off the 'paci' on my jeans. With the third, I shoved it back in the baby's mouth, usually after the dog had a chance to lick it."

Having subsequent children teaches moms and dads to adopt a "whatever works" mentality. After all, with two or more small children swarming your hive, you may be willing to incur later dentist bills and let your babe take a bottle to bed. A warped adult may be the least of your worries when night after night your toddler climbs into your bed, scared of the monsters in his closet.

A sage mom, one of my mentors, once told me how her father-in-law frowned to see his grandson standing on the coffee table to reach something on a shelf. Given that Mom's attention was so often on her baby daughter, she brushed this disapproval off as if it were lint. "Around here, Dad," she said, "we do whatever works."

Don't wait until a second child or a crisis hits to enjoy the wisdom of "whatever works." What a gift it is to those you love, when you dispense with formalities and make your home a comfortable place to be human. Learn that traditions are meant to be broken and recast, and that love and support for one another always takes precedence.

Mommy Experts Tell You How to Get Your Spouse to Lift a Finger

"Make lists of all the specifics you handle. Highlight the highest priorities. Renegotiate."

"Write a plan and post it prominently in the house. Revisit priorities often."

"Leave the baby with him for several hours at a time, from the earliest age possible."

"Acknowledge his breadwinning. Catch him doing something good and compliment him."

"Give him a job, say being in charge of bedtime—baths, teeth, stories, and all."

"Try not to interfere, no matter how poorly he's doing something."

"Drop your standards dramatically. Expect him to leave tasks somewhat undone, and less than perfectly done."

"Reward help with sex."

"Get kids involved in household work, too."

chapter ten

Sex in the Minivan

Finding Time (and Desire) for Love

> SECRET: *Romance suffers during these years but you can* lure *pleasure from its hiding place.*

There used to be drums. Making love to my husband, my mind traveled to places with percussion. The tang of a *mojito* on my tongue, a drummer wore a ruffled shirt in a Havana nightclub in the '50s. Condensation rings the water glasses of a packed blues bar where hips take on a life of their own. A waiter peeled a whole orange in one long, curling strip in Sevilla, where every breeze smelled of citrus trees. Hula on the lanai at the five-star Haleku-lani Hotel, plumeria floated in a bowl, and the tide came in with the sunset.

Since I've had children, however, I don't hear the drums. When Duke holds me close, I am entirely too present in my bedroom, travel-ing only as far as the folded clothes that need to be put away, library books on the dresser that are coming due, and school permission slips I remind myself to sign. Exotic climes, pulsing music, and perfumes have given way to blemished backs, perfunctory kisses, and a prerecorded narrator in my head saying, "You need to do this for him."

How I miss her: that woman who could lose herself; the one comfortable enough with herself she could tell him how, where, and when; and her desire, sleepy sometimes but often easily roused. I went outside my body, confident in the way only love and passion can make you, and was transfixed by the fact that my husband, this generous soul with the broad shoulders and taut belly could love me so.

One humid afternoon near a lake in the Canadian Rockies where Duke and I spent our honeymoon, my body couldn't get *there,* that place I was determined to go. And NOBODY was leaving that cabin until I got there. That's how fierce I once was about my own pleasure, which today I regard as negligible.

When I got pregnant, Duke puffed up with the pride of a stud, his notion that all that infertility nonsense could be forgotten with a few nights with him. The second trimester hormones were great drugs, too, and we were as happy and busy as rabbits. And although we referred to it as "Duke having sex," we willed labor to start with a strange manipulation of accessible body parts.

From Libertine to Schoolmarm

Those of you saying "Eeewww," including my boys who will one day check out this chapter as teenagers, can nevertheless see Duke and I were not inhibited by taboos. In Boston, where I spent my single years, I was the sole Protestant and a Presbyterian minister's daughter nonetheless among a circle of Catholic friends. For that reason, I guess, I was often consulted about orgasms and other liberating acts my friends weren't sure fit into a semi-religious persona. I was not terribly experienced when I got married, but my attitude seemed progressive among guilt-ridden women in an intellectual's city not known for its steamy side.

When I moved to Southern California, where considerably less clothing is worn year-round and lawn chairs become passion pits, I didn't expect to be anyone's Dr. Ruth. And after settling into the twice and occasionally thrice-per-week routine of married life, I confess the brazen and detailed brunch chats on *Sex and the City* intimidated me.

Nevertheless, after having two babies and wandering into a counselor's office for a little talk about my lack of libido, I wasn't prepared for the grade I'd get on a sexual growth chart. When the counselor asked me if I knew what "turned me on," I wrinkled my nose and said, "I can't describe it using *that* term." A person seduced by words, I had a shortlist of acceptable names for sexual things—neat compromises between too-graphic and too schmaltzy. However, the counselor viewed my truncated sexual vocabulary as a sign that I was prim and suppressed—a diagnosis that, frankly, felled me from my chair.

For those of us who think of ourselves as passion kittens, the postpartum reality is often macaroni-and-cheese bland. For those of us waiting for the long advertised sexual peak, only to find occasional divots in an otherwise flat landscape, it's a sorry state of affairs. Because even the friend of mine who picked "Lola" as a pseudonym for use in this book, isn't getting any and couldn't care less.

Before she was married, Lola enjoyed an active sexual life in which she slept with about 100 men. But now the mother of two, Lola says, "I never want to have sex again." She and her husband recently bought a king-sized bed, so that they could watch *Willy Wonka and the Chocolate Factory* snuggled up with their two- and four-year-olds. "After having children, sex just feels too visceral. Like when I was nursing, I didn't want the babies to smell sex on me."

Lola says it isn't a stale sex life that's to blame. "I see cute guys now, and I can't even get excited thinking about sex with strangers. I have body issues galore. And absolutely no interest."

Aimee chimes in at a mompool, explaining that she learned in recovery from alcoholism to "think a drink through." The same applies to sex, she says. "If I think the sex through, I think of getting pregnant again, of being tied to the house with another baby, of being so exhausted I can't take care of my other kids. And my husband will still be useless while I'm doing everything."

What a twist: It's actually cooler at this life juncture to divulge how *little* sex you're having than how much. This isn't true for all new mothers. Single moms who aren't in romantic relationships don't have to "think it through," they *welcome* more action. And women new to being stepmoms appear frisky and fulfilled, noting no change in their love lives from before they took on at least a part-time, part-way parenting responsibility.

But married moms with babies through five-year-olds tell me there are as many reasons not to have sex as there are nights on the calendar: exhaustion, leaky breasts from breast-feeding, residual pain from giving birth, lack of desire, inability to relax, fear of pregnancy, difficulty climaxing, resentment of husbands, boredom with the bedroom routine, worry the kids will interrupt or hear, feeling spent from the physicality of motherhood, feeling "mothers don't do this," and self consciousness about weight, stretch marks, saggy breasts, and the like. One mom laughs, "I just don't want to have to take a shower." In a similar vein, another says, "I don't have the energy to change the sheets."

In fact, the problem is so multilayered that no matter how many silk scarves you seductively pull away, the center remains covered up. Sex used to be so easy, so mindless. Now it's a scheduling nightmare. A chemistry test. And synchronized desire? Forget about it.

Moms in the immediate aftermath of birth are glad for the six-week reprieve from sex that doctors recommend. Those who jump the gun and even some who wait a few weeks more, find intercourse painful. Breast-feeding moms trying to be courtesans describe milk shooting out of them and across the room, and breasts too full they hurt or too empty they sag and sway. They talk about how the bone-dry environs of their vaginas aren't hospitable. Or they are disgusted by babies and husbands handling the same nipples.

It's Not Just You

Men in this stage can experience decreased drive as well—and not just because they're too tired to get it up, or recovering from the sight of the gory afterbirth. Scientists have learned that similar to their wives, male partners experience increases in estrogen before babies are born and drops in testosterone in the weeks thereafter. Indeed, the longer males in the research study held their newborns, the greater their drop in that sex-craving drug testosterone. As if we needed *another* reason for Dad to pitch in more, it turns out holding babies is like putting a little saltpeter in his tea.

It's also a strange new world: the notion of being lovers and parents. A baby in a bassinet in Mom and Dad's bedroom might be wakened or warped by grunts or moans made in the dark. An intercom-broadcast baby cough or squeak could turn a hot mama cold, as could the thought of the waiting laundry, the sight of a ticking alarm clock, or the report you were supposed to have couriered before you left the office. Passionate moves and positions that once seemed so natural and fluid now seem to take place in a lit incubator with a class of kindergarteners looking on with curious anticipation.

The Politics of Feeling Good

In marriages that never thrived on sex, post-kid couples still hum happily along without much. But even in marriages in which making love was a kind of glue for the relationship, postnatal passion gets the short shrift.

Women who tell me they go weeks, even a month or more, without sex are common; some dread the next time they have to engage in it. They seem to have folded and packed away their sexuality with their prom dresses and working girl suits—mementos that from that point on, they only visit on occasion.

Moms who still dress up and go to work each day are more likely to feel sexy than moms who stay home. But both sets are way too tired to rally after their children are tucked in. Moms experiencing postpartum depression don't want sex. And moms on antidepressants want to romp but can't climax, which makes them stop wanting to.

Many moms seem to rebound two or three years after having a baby, and want sex a couple times a month. Exercises to tighten pelvic muscles called "kegels" help women who can't fathom sex will ever be the same after being stretched from here to eternity to birth an eight-pound babe. To have an orgasm, some say they require more vigorous and targeted stimulation of the clitoris than before birth.

Strategies to ease sex-impinging tension are much harder to come by. Some women feel they need to shake off their mommy persona before they can "let go." Many suggest a glass of wine or two helps sometimes, if a mom is rested and mid-menstrual cycle—in other words, vaguely frisky. My friend Suzanne needs an hour-long massage before she can be in the mood, and her benevolent husband obliges. Other moms have to have hotel rooms and at least a weekend's length of downtime. Saturday and Sunday mornings are favored by the crowd with kids old enough to get their own cereal and turn on cartoons.

Ideally, moms say they want more foreplay. Of course, the best foreplay of all is a hunk doing his share of household work: a husband who does middle of the night feedings or tuck-ins. A husband who cooks dinner (with vegetables)! A husband who takes the baby and tells Mom to "go out, get a manicure, and buy something nice for herself." These are a new mom's Chippendales.

Mercy Sex and Quickies

However, many women subscribe to "mercy sex" designed only to quell a husband's need, or quickies for practicality's sake. Once engaged in parenthood, hubbies often want a more active sex life than their wives do, an uncomfortable discrepancy in a phase of marriage already prone to distance and strain.

Men whose romantic initiatives are frequently denied take this harder than most wives imagine. Because as frustrating as this fact is, men need icing before they can make cake whereas women need cake to even *want* some frosting. In other words, sex is a man's route to intimacy while for women, sex is a by-product of intimacy.

Moms tend to think sex should be the least of their worries during this stressful passage. And that husbands are incredibly selfish to expect regular sex, knowing how physically draining motherhood is and how little of us is left over in this intense stage. Relentless youngsters paw at us twelve to fifteen hours a day. Then our husbands turn to us with their seemingly insatiable need. It's infuriating that men can't turn down their desire as we can when crunch or crisis times hit.

Dads, on the other hand, feel that since the baby came along, they've sunk lower in priority on the totem pole than the family dog. They believe they deserve the extra attention and can't jive with us on thinking of sex as a luxury item, or a drain on one's energy. Their physiology mandates that sex is a necessity, and intercourse loosens them up to a degree they can't otherwise achieve—even if left to their own devices in the shower.

Parenthood, however, is much newer to moms than the incorrigible penis. So we immerse ourselves in understanding a baby's physiology and how to meet the momentous needs of our developing child. The last thing on our minds is the need to understand better our big lug's sex drive or his biological build. But in a situation ripe for misunderstandings, with repercussions that are devastating to needy husbands, you may benefit from a refresher course on the strange truths of male sexuality.

Is He Incredibly Selfish?

Marriage therapists Melissa McBurney and Louis McBurney, M.D., work together, counseling couples at the Marble Retreat in Marble, Colorado. Melissa says the book *The Sexual Man* by Dr. Archibald D. Hart, is the best guide to grasping the psyche men bring to the bedroom. Of her own awakening as a wife, Melissa notes that once she better understood what men need, it changed her attitude about their sex life. In an Internet column, she says, "I hadn't realized, for instance, that being sexually satisfied greatly influences Louis's ability to perform at work . . . [With that realization] I stopped seeing Louis's sexual need, which was higher than my own, as totally selfish."

Have you ever tried to imagine feeling the physical longings your husband describes—how physically pent-up he gets when it's been a while since he's popped his cork? A couple times I've tried to emulate this mounting tension by walking around with a near-bursting bladder, or by holding back a sneeze. Moms who nurse have a closer analogy, with a breast that grows rock-hard and achy if a feeding runs late. Merely by applying this prism, you begin to put yourself in your husband's pants and see his need as something other than a narcissist's craving for entertainment. With a smidge more compassion, you may choose to reframe your whole carnal outlook, seeing ways in which you can show him love, improve his mood, and give him more energy for all aspects of your lives.

Biases About Moms and Sex

To further complicate matters, a woman is susceptible to big changes in her sexual outlook when she becomes a mother, which isn't always a high priority for her to sort out. The intensive mothering mind-set drives many previously well-rounded individuals to abandon their own desires for the sake of their kids. As we've seen, moms are made to feel selfish for wanting full lives, active sex lives being the most superfluous of the sacrifices we are expected to make.

At a picnic on the patio I hosted for a couple of families last year, a friend revealed her mommy biases, which I believe are still pervasive in our culture. "I don't think moms should wear sundresses that revealing," a friend said disapprovingly of another guest. At a mall another day, the same friend disparaged a pregnant woman whose stomach was bared in a midriff—this, from a seemingly progressive thinker who was a free-wheeling, sexual engine during her single years.

I would never have guessed I was capable of such stereotypes either. But delving into my maternal inhibitions, I found that orgasms were right up there with time with friends, exercise and, hobbies—things I believed new mothers sacrificed.

My mom, a Mary Tyler Moore lookalike and a hottie in capris during the '60s, is mad for my dad. But never had I walked in on my parents in the act, nor given much thought to my mom being evolved in every way. I knew I never wanted to be in the position a friend of mine was, when her ten-year-old daughter asked, "Mommy, was Daddy hurting you when he made you scream so loud last night?"

Believe it or not, at the age of thirty-nine, it finally dawned on me why my parents played classical music so loud in their bedroom at night, and why they insisted on sleeping with a fan on even in the dead of a Missouri winter. Duh . . . mommies had sex!

Bliss Is Your Birthright

Knowing that as a mom, bliss is your birthright is nevertheless a far cry from actualizing it in a pimpled relationship—one in which your husband has abundant energy for the horizontal bop but none for cleaning the dinner dishes, one in which he is needlessly gruff to his son but whispers sweet innuendos to you. It's often impossible to sweep aside the clean laundry stacked on the bed and the resentment it represents, even if you want your just reward between the sheets.

But don't blow off your own pleasure as a means of getting back at him. It's best in this case to aim for conquest, not consummation. If possible, negotiate dish duty *after* you've served yourself a little helping of heaven. He will be more amenable when he's satisfied, and having experienced some release of your own, you'll likely complain in softer tones.

Don't resort to "just get it over with" sex week after week. Over time, sex therapists say, a woman who eschews or doesn't achieve orgasms is doomed to become less interested in sex and to gradually decrease the lengths to which she will let passion go. The emotional repercussions are also serious. For awhile, it's fine getting bonked, lying there lifeless as a Lincoln Log. Eventually though, you can't concede. You begin to feel violated for saying yes, when you really, *really* mean no.

Take These Suggestions to Bed!

Now that I've played out these cheery sex scenes for you, I can hope your relationship has not come to this. I can hope you've lassoed your libido and taken your husband out for a ride. But if your love life resembles these pages more than those of an erotic novel, you'll be glad for the suggestions my girlfriends and I have in store. Take these ideas to heart, and then, on the double, take them to bed!

Let Me Hear Your Body Talk

Before you blast me for dredging up the worst of Olivia Newton John's repertoire, hear me out. You need to get attuned to your body—you know, the one underneath those baggy clothes, the one you hold in contempt, the one you hope never again to see naked in daylight. Start treating yourself to healthier habits.

Until you feel better about yourself, you won't feel nerve endings tingle, you won't see the grace in your curves, or the way your lusty husband adores you. For some women, the emotional turning point in parenthood comes when they return to the gym and start getting their pre-baby bodies back.

Get Your Body Moving

As bitter as I was in my early motherhood months about skinny mini author Vicki Iovine telling me to exercise in *The Girlfriends' Guide to Having a Baby,* I do believe that walking, especially with a friend, is the antidote to much of what ails us. Yoga, too, many moms report, gave them rare moments of relief from muscle tension and the shallow breathing a baby's cries can bring on.

Moms who are depressed will attest that even if there is a will, there is sometimes not a way. But if you can get moving, even for just a couple blocks at first, the benefits to your cranky mood, your screwed-up psyche, your spacey mommy brain, your aching back, your sluggish metabolism, your baby belly, your sensual self, and to the little one who accompanies you in a baby jogger or stroller are immense.

Eat Right and Sleep More

For me, my husband's homegrown tomatoes and herb garden are also aphrodisiacs. Who knew that salad could be so sensual? But when I eat better and concentrate on giving my body the nutrients and the water it needs to function optimally—as a mother would do for her child—I reap a gazillion rewards. I feel lighter and less self-conscious about the stubborn pounds aging and childbirth have put on me. I feel connected to the single part of me that lived in the Italian North End of Boston, shopping European style at cheese shops and fruit and vegetable stands, and savoring red wine with meals.

Seeing food the sensual way that the Italians do, your body feels more like a temple, a place to be honored and tickled and lit up with celebration.

Slumber, too, is sexy. Graduate your bed to the highest thread count or make your sanctuary off limits to kids eating ice cream or trading Yu-Gi-Oh! cards. Once per quarter if possible, go away for a weekend with nothing on the agenda but sleep. My girlfriends and I can almost guarantee that once you are rested, you'll feel like burning some energy with a little bump and grind.

Feel Good in and Out of Clothes

Buy clothes that fit well, rather than squeezing yourself into too-small jeans or knits that emphasize flaws. Check *What Not to Wear* out from the library, for expert tips on disguising body flaws. Get a makeover, with an emphasis on fast and easy ways to feel pretty.

Even more important, get massages. There's nothing as healing for a mom than being treated to an hour of touch—touch that is purely about your health and well-being and makes no demands of you. It's also hard to hate a body into which someone quiet and curative has rubbed lavender essence and taken such care to nurture.

Talk About Sex

Clear out emotional cobwebs in conversation with your spouse. Consider and then articulate your new feelings about sex. Be specific about the origins of the reluctance you feel, for example saying, "I feel overburdened by the housework and am less apt to want to 'do it' with you when you won't share the chores." Or, explain that hormonally or otherwise, you don't yet feel like yourself, an admission that will relieve his sense of being an ineffective or unattractive lover.

Listening to your body, you may find you need a respite from sex and must ask your partner not to make demands during this time. Acknowledge his need for relief from physical pressure, and he will be much more likely to accept your need for relief from psychological pressure. As it did for my friend Suzanne, the one whose magnanimous hubby provides hourlong, full-body massages before sex, this conversation may persuade your husband to brush up on his technique and find better ways to help you relax.

Seek Help. Your Libido's Important!

If you pay more attention to your health—mental, emotional, and physical—and feel your equilibrium is still way off, seek help. Vitamins or herbal remedies might boost your mood. Your doctor can also run blood tests to measure estrogen and testosterone levels, evaluate you for desire-sapping depression or anxiety, or pinpoint and treat injuries from childbirth that make sex painful or uncomfortable. Don't let sexual delight slip away without exploring possible underlying medical complications.

All this said, there's still a big mind-shift to make on behalf of your sexual self. After you've tackled the physiologic minefields, it's onto the psychological ones.

Take Responsibility for Your Own Libido

I've seen the play *The Vagina Monologues* twice. I went to a women's college. I spent formative years being taught how empowering it is to know one's own body, to name the red folds of skin usually buried in my underwear, and of finding out for myself what I specifically need and want from a lover. But like most women, I still thought of libido as this mysterious maiden who sometimes slinks out to dance on tables at a bar, who sometimes can be teased out by a charming talker or a good kisser, and who retreats into her cave at times for weeks on end.

Until I started mourning her lengthy disappearance, I didn't realize libido was mine to locate, evoke, and master. I'd looked to Duke to seduce her, to improve his technique at chasing her down. I'd blamed hormones, I'd blamed being overworked and tired, I'd found external reasons for not wanting to experience transcendent joy. I had not looked within.

Mind you, my husband and I tried *everything* to track the source of my disinterest. There was the "only when Marg initiates" experiment that lasted several months, bursting out of the starting gate only to slow in subsequent outings. There was appointment-only sex, calendared in with the intent of making us salivate but which put a lot of pressure on Tuesdays.

Testosterone cream, which in my case was applied to the inside of the wrist like a French perfume, bombed big time, and Viagra for me—even purchased for cheap at Costco—proved a waste of money without the engorgement and badda bing! it promised.

Marriage counseling intent on removing relationship barriers taught us some better ways to communicate but didn't coax the maiden to run across the moors. Friends said I was harboring anger, but on rare weekends away with Duke, I could re-enact great love scenes of our past, and I remembered so much of what I had always adored about him.

For the sake of more regular romps, we tried other tactics, too. Phone sex was an utter travesty; I sounded like a bad actor at an audition, putting the inflection on all the wrong syllables. Devices needed as many batteries as my boys' remote control cars. Lingerie was unthinkable, and wine sufficient enough to loosen the tongue made me fall asleep on the sofa. Trysts during lunch breaks, out on dates, even in the minivan, did amp up the excitement but the positions weren't ideal.

You can see how dogged Duke and I were in search of the

maiden, in search of my feisty spirit, in search of the drums that made my marriage beat wildly and well. Fortunately, most moms I know don't have to look as high and low; their desire can be coaxed with fewer of these high-jinks. But for me, my passionate prerequisite was as elusive as could be.

Sensual Sensations

My turning point came in two's. First, my counselor made me go back to basics, as if I were a guileless teenager discovering my sensuality anew. I had to listen to my body all day long, when I moved and exercised, when I showered or crossed my legs, noting even the tiniest flicker of sexual feeling. I had to start perusing the landscape for any trigger of good sensations: white and pink cabbage roses, faded jeans, spa robes, merlots legging down a wine glass, cute men with their ties loosened, drippy candelabras, Adam's apples, jet streams in hot tubs, and coat closets at fancy hotels. I forced myself to check erotica out of the library; I stayed awake through a lesbian porn film. I tried to push the limits of prudishness, to check out things that were a few steps beyond my comfort zone without violating the cardinal rule of "what felt good to me."

Communing with good sensations made me feel sexual again. An inner life is where you'll find libido, the lark who relies on you to notice and give emphasis to her amid distractions, and who wants to be integral to the woman you are, if you'll only make way now and then.

Happiness Restores Libido

Secondly, Duke and I found a way for me to start writing again. I went away one night every month to write the proposal and the first chapters of this book. I stayed with my dear single friend Lucy who plied me with wine and great meals, and turned her home over to my muse. I learned that in me, the muse and my libido are bosom buddies. Once my creativity was loosed again on the page, I was loosed again on my husband. And at my fortieth birthday brunch, a girls-only event, I regaled a long table of friends with stories of revived passions, my glow brighter than forty candles. A book contract, and lots of other new chapters, lay ahead of me in life.

If that glow is important to you, or even if you've decided it isn't, go within to look for the reasons. Take ownership of your libidos, and let mommies everywhere enjoy all that life offers us.

Make Risky Whoopie

Risks come in all shapes and sizes. And as I've described above, there are plenty of risks that lie readily accessible on the Saturn rings of your comfort zone. And taking risks as a married woman and a responsible mother doesn't mean you break your vows or compromise your worthiness of respect.

But mommies need risks, the same way they need secret lives and quiet indulgences, the same way we need to expose our humanness and the less-than-perfect world in which we mother. A transfusion of little dares makes you feel your children are not the only ones growing, not the only ones getting zinged by the excitement of learning new things.

So, Denver mom Dalia challenges you to try morning sex, even if you are not a morning person. She put spark back in her monotonous love life, by shifting to a bright daylight, eyes-wide-open routine she never before embraced. Last week, already dressed for work with fifteen minutes to get to a morning meeting, Dalia pushed her coffee-savoring husband into the bedroom and threw panty hose and schedules to the wind. "Act the instant you get the urge, because the urge is often too fleeting to wait."

Dalia is also a vision in leather jackets and streamlined Nordstrom skirts these days, having lost more than sixty pounds on Weight Watchers over the last year. Taking her sweet time, losing at most two pounds a week, Dalia has plowed through plateaus, eating binges, and enormous self-doubt to feel like a sexual creature again.

Mom-Sized Risks

Another friend of mine has just joined a band, and although she's singing Elton John songs and not the torch songs she'd prefer, Liza is making her *American Idol* side-dream come true. Another mommy friend of mine just christened her stretched abdomen with a belly button ring.

Tall bushes on a neighborhood street and tinted windows in minivans make great camouflage. Have you shared a cigar on the roof of your office building at midnight? Remember sex behind the bleachers? This time, try a buffet table with a ground-sweeping tablecloth, abandoned from an earlier wedding or graduation. In this impromptu tent, you may have some of the most outrageous sex you've ever quietly and itchingly performed.

There's certainly nothing wrong with vicariously enjoying a friend-of-a-friend's tales from her swinger marriage. Some La Jolla, California, housewives shocked me last year, telling me about Christmas exchanges of vibrators and clauses in their marriages that allowed them free rein with lovers of their own gender. Far outside my comfort zone, sitting with this crowd reestablished boundaries for me. And I safely snared a couple technical pointers they revealed from their sexual encounters that I could go home and share with Duke.

Titillating Time Away

One of the biggest risks in early motherhood is that of traveling and leaving small kids behind with relatives or babysitters. Many women are too worried or too attached to their kids to go away for a weekend, much less a week. But last year, prompted by a dear friend's invitation to come to her wedding on Scotland's Isle of Skye, Duke and I left our boys behind for ten days and devoted ourselves to pubs, kilts, and makeout sessions in the alleys of London and outside whiskey distilleries in Scotland. Colin Firth accents and Wuthering Heights bogs are my undoing, as is any time my husband gets me out of town. We carry the heady stoke of that trip to this day. Our boys got alone time with grandparents, repeated trips to Chuck E. Cheese from a babysitter who could tolerate it, and big presents from Harrods to boot.

I should add that weekly date nights with your husband do not fall into the risk category because they are necessities. Make time for your marriage, even if it's to grocery shop together or read books side by side in a café.

Then go one step beyond and do the unthinkable: buy a matching set of bra and underwear. Arrange a midweek picnic at a rose garden. Tuck your husband in with a bedtime story of your own making. Dare him to serenade you below your bedroom window next Mother's Day.

Let your wild roots sprout again in the soil of motherhood. Don't just ensure that your child gets a full range of life experiences; treat yourself. Stop expecting percussion to be played from the wings, and start playing your own bass beat. Tethered to a fun, healthy family life, keep your own lifelines alive and sprawling in the atmosphere of savory adventures and unexpected encounters.

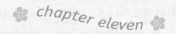

chapter eleven

Crisis Management at Home

Dealing with the Unthinkable—and Emerging Stronger Than Ever

> SECRET: *Good people and good marriages can get waylaid by stress. Instead of turning on each other, be a team.*

Sarah, a mother in Houston, had no idea before giving birth to her daughter that her husband had a problem with her putting on some weight. In her mid-thirties, Sarah found it difficult to lose the twenty pounds left over after giving birth and during more than a year of breast-feeding her daughter. She was crushed by Greg's admission that Sarah's extra weight made her less sexually appealing.

Meanwhile at work, Greg was assigned a new partner, a svelte young woman who was the prototype woman to whom he was attracted. Sarah had already experienced a plunge in self-esteem, taking a break from her established career as one of Houston's foremost massage therapists to care for their baby. And the punches just kept coming, word of this bombshell at Greg's office deepening her fears and anxieties, at a time when she could barely keep up with their colicky baby's demands.

Sarah's weight went up and down, as she tried The Zone diet

and then Weight Watchers, oscillated between intense exercise regimens and exhaustion, and between eating only vegetables to feeding her sadness handfuls of sweets. Attempts to reason with Greg often failed, as he disliked confrontation and grew nasty in arguments.

Two years later, their blond daughter leads Sarah and Greg on walks in the evenings and it's clear their marriage has weathered the storm. "I know a lot of men feel the way Greg did," says Sarah, who shed weight, but on her own terms, so that she now feels good about herself. "I wish Greg had not been so brutally honest about the weight issues." Wanting her marriage to last, she said, "I sought the counsel of a lot of my former clients, women who I knew were married to similar men. And I learned how to distance myself from certain things that were said, and to approach my husband differently when problems came up."

A bundle of joy can also be a bundle of crises. The baby isn't to blame, of course, but many times neither are we, caught off guard by strange feelings that emerge in this transition and by our response to duress.

When Stress Turns Couples Against Each Other

Indeed, a marriage counselor once told Duke and me that couples exposed to high degrees of stress respond the same way lab rats do. In the scientific experiment, she explained, rats received electric shocks while in a cage. "At first, the rats tried desperately to find a way out, pawing and trying to climb the walls of their cage," she said. "Then, when they found they couldn't escape, they turned on each other. They started fighting bitterly."

Duke and I left that appointment very sober. In statistics she'd quoted, most parents didn't regain their former level of marital satisfaction until their kids grew up and left home, some twenty years later.

Prior to becoming parents, Duke and I thought we had a splendid marriage, good enough to publish a book about. We groomed ourselves to join the one-third of marriages that sail through the parenthood blockade, peaceful and unscathed. But like Sarah and Greg, we had our comeuppance.

One evening I came home from my hospital marketing job with a migraine and closed myself up in the bedroom with all the lights off. Patrick and Liam were tender with me, bringing cold towels for my forehead, talking in whisper-volumes they have not used since. Come bedtime though, they did not want to be apart from me, and Duke brusquely tried to herd them alone, to Liam's screaming refrains.

Nauseated and dizzy, I got out of bed and stormed into their room to rescue them from their inpatient father yet again. It was then I saw Duke trying to stifle Liam's shouts, his hands over my little boy's mouth in a way that scared me out of my wits. I pulled Liam away and hit Duke with my palms, and in the insanity of that moment, Duke hit me back, not hard, but a hit nonetheless.

My migraine made it possible only for me to get the kids safely tucked in and then stumble back to bed. But the intense sadness and shame that two people who loved each other so much could be moved to hitting one another, lingered for days.

The first chance I had, I confessed this abomination to my sister. I was at the grocery store on the cell phone, with aisles full of shoppers as an added audience. Having been married longer than I have, and more practical by nature, Catherine was nonplussed by my secret. As I held open an egg carton and inspected the fragile family inside, Catherine filled my cell phone with cheer, and with the reassurance that this account represented nothing but another zany day in paradise.

The Unthinkable Is Not Unusual

Upon my disclosures, several other friends—one in an almost fifty-year marriage—related stories in which they had physically skirmished, shoving and slapping at each other. And I realized that the unimaginable was in fact, not so uncommon. In remote instances of extreme stress and emotion, husbands and wives who were nevertheless in love and intact as married couples had resorted to physical force.

We were, in essence, no different than rats. Filled with the same fight-or-flight response as endangered animals, our vows made us resist the urge to run. But fight? Well, with heart rates soaring, lungs full to bursting, and muscles readied with blood, we did what our bodies were designed to do in such extreme circumstances: We lunged at the only visible foe.

I found this astonishing, that marriages could sink lower than low and survive. Except that couples who emerged from the dark side brushed the horror off my shoulders and set me walking again, back into the lion's den of my life. They suggested that even the most disparate partners could be brought together into a team, when they decide their love is too important to allow stress to divide and conquer it.

What do you do when the unthinkable occurs? When your marriage sours so dramatically that you're no longer sold on the whole institution of marriage? I asked mothers who experienced unspeakable horrors—from affairs to sick kids to personal demons. They lived through and negotiated the unimaginable pain, and have wisdom aplenty to share.

While these examples make weight gain and pansy punches seem tame, the bigger crises these moms endured contain the same elements of exhaustion, blame, confusion, vulnerability, pain, shock, and worry that wrack new moms and dads in day-to-day life. If they can emerge strong and whole, which all of them have, we surely can, too.

Elizabeth's Story: Affair and Abandonment

My friend Elizabeth from Marin County, north of San Francisco, believes her husband started having an affair when she was pregnant with their second child. It was a time of calamity for Evan, Elizabeth says, because he'd lost his job the year before, was struggling to make a going concern of the business he'd started, and enormous debt was mounting. With their new baby coming, Elizabeth proposed they sell their house, get out from under their debt, and start over—a prospect that sent Evan reeling.

Their newborn daughter, Mackensie, was sickly, having been diagnosed with a milk protein allergy and a condition that required the baby to wear an uncomfortable brace that disturbed her sleep. Elizabeth's hands were more than full, managing the care of Mackensie and her three-year-old brother, Brian, and working full-time at the high-powered administrative job that kept the family afloat. So it was an unfathomable blow when Evan came home one evening and announced that he was leaving his family and moving in with his secretary, the new love of his life.

Elizabeth proposed counseling in hopes of staving off the end of their twelve-year marriage. But Evan would not return or recoup the marriage, leaving Elizabeth with all the accumulated debt in addition to being a single mother with two small children.

Elizabeth is not proud of having been so enraged that she

subsequently rammed her car into Evan's car in the driveway of his new home. Yet, everyone marvels at how she overcame this terrible betrayal and went on to raise two genuinely extraordinary kids. Although she lost her house and it took years of savings, and battles over child support, to afford another home, Elizabeth is gearing up for her next big challenge—stashing away money for Ivy League educations for which her super-smart kids, now in middle school and high school, are destined.

Amanda's Story: A Terrible Accident

It could have been a cocoa commercial. One Saturday in March when her four-year-old came in from sledding in the backyard, Amanda helped Justin out of his wet clothes and put a kettle of milk on their electric stovetop to make hot chocolate. A cautious, thoughtful kid, Justin told his mom he would wait in the kitchen and watch for the steam to rise while Amanda took clean laundry upstairs.

In a few minutes, Justin's eight-year-old brother and sledding mate came indoors and started shedding their layers, which Amanda and her husband, Joe, heard from upstairs. But the next sound was a shriek, followed by Justin's brother shouting for Mom and Dad to come quick because Justin was on fire.

In a situation in which even a second's passing is critical, Joe rushed down the stairs, already peeling off his sweatshirt, and threw it onto Justin, whose T-shirt had burned completely off his back. After wrapping his back in wet washcloths and slipping him carefully into a bathrobe, Amanda laid Justin in the backseat of their van, resting his head on her lap for the quick trip to the emergency room in the small town in Minnesota where they live.

The triage nurse took one look at Justin and rushed the family into a treatment room, where an intravenous line was started before the medical team even asked for the boy's name. It wasn't until the doctors said Justin would need to be transferred by ambulance to a hospital with a specialized burn unit that Joe and Amanda realized how serious the accident was.

Justin had suffered third-degree burns across his back and under his armpit. In an out-of-character move for their son, Amanda and Joe told the doctors, Justin had apparently climbed a kitchen stool and scooted next to the stovetop, where his loose T-shirt lodged under an electric burner and started the fire.

The family's pastor got wind of the accident, tracked them down in this distant hospital's intensive care unit, and drove two hours to be with them that terrifying first night. Justin had lost nerve cell endings, so he was not in pain but would need a skin graft and face a dangerous and difficult recovery.

"Our pastor held his hand over Justin's hospital bed as he prayed. And I remember him saying how thankful we were that Justin had been spared, which was when I started to cry. Somehow hearing that our son could have died was so much more real in a prayer that it was in a statement. When the pastor hugged me, it took a long time for me to let him go."

Following Justin's hospitalization, three months of three-times-a-day dressing changes were required at home. These procedures were cumbersome, infection-prone, and emotionally explosive because the nerve cells were regenerating and touching Justin caused him great pain. Amanda says that peeling dead skin off her four-year-old's back, applying jars full of gooey ointment, bandages, gauze, and outer wrappings was bad but not nearly as bad as addressing the dread and screams the onset of every dressing change inspired.

Eventually, the raw wounds did close and heal, and Justin regained his full mobility and strength, although he will always have textured scars covering his back and have to keep them out of the sun.

Mother to the "burned kid" in a Mayberrylike small town, Amanda was cognizant of whispers and people who suggested that she and Joe were somehow at fault for this mishap. On the flip side, talking about the accident made Amanda a member of a club she says she never wanted to be a part of but that "proved full of incredible women, dozens of whom came up to me and shared freak accidents or profound setbacks in their families."

During this entire time, Amanda and Joe never turned on each other. "Maybe because we were together when it happened, it never came to that," Amanda relates. Instead, they focused on preventing the accident from stigmatizing their sons. Days after the accident, they had to reassure Justin's eight-year-old brother who berated himself for not remembering "Stop, drop, and roll." Justin, too, got so sick of people asking him if he was all right, and hated anyone to see his scars. A change in schools meant Justin could rejoice that not a single kid in his class knew about the accident. By the end of the summer, the family took a deep breath and decided not to forego their long-planned trip to the Dakota foothills. Vacation photos show their family of four at the summit, triumph in the outer tips of their smiles.

Sally Jean's Story: Teenage Mothers Grow Up

Having had three children by three different fathers, Sally Jean offered her stories by phone from Columbus, Ohio, eagerly and un-self-consciously, when I posted a solicitation for mommies' accounts on Internet sites. "I first got pregnant at age fifteen," she says, "so I don't pull any punches with young women. I tell them, don't have kids. You may think you want kids but you really don't unless you've graduated from college, you're married, and the marriage is right."

Sally Jean married the father of her first son, only to have him leave her for another girl, which launched the series of homes she set up, first at her mother's then at a grandmother's. When her grandmother could no longer afford to have her and the baby there, Sally Jean found herself on the streets with no money and a five-month-old. "We slept in a friend's car. I breast-fed him, eating out of the garbage to keep my milk supply going. It was right before Christmas, there was snow on the ground, and it was freezing cold. No one ever told me I was going to be in a situation like this."

Sally Jean admits she's made many mistakes and doesn't think she should ever have had children so young. Collecting welfare, as she did for four years, "I screwed up my first son, Jonathan, so badly. I was out every weekend partying. I'd line up babysitters, hell, I had babysitters for my babysitters. I was the person who messed up my son's life when I was the one who was supposed to protect him."

Arrested amid her partying and drinking, Sally Jean subsequently lost custody of Jonathan to her former husband, with whom the boy has now lived for nine years except for summers when he visits Sally Jean and her family. "He has ADHD, he feels like he's stupid. He has emotional problems and feels as if nobody loves him. I cry myself to sleep every night, knowing what a terrible thing I have done. And I call Jonathan every day; I have to, I'm his mother. I need to tell him I love him. And this nine-year-old always tells me how proud he is of me, how proud he is that I have straightened out my life."

It's clear the more we talk that Jonathan is coming through the troubles all right and is being rebuilt by divorced parents who grew up a little, made a plan, and dramatically improved his care and love. Yet, Sally Jean beats herself up constantly for being young and foolish and failing him.

She never yells at her other two children, she says, and loves them immensely. Many nights, though, she stays up almost all night cleaning her house, washing down the walls, and rearranging the furniture. "My doctor says I'm too hard on myself and that I have to push forward and stop looking back. But I don't know how you ever really get over putting a baby in that position."

Thinking of Sally Jean cleaning compulsively, trying to cleanse herself, I imagine, of memories that become all too vivid at night, it remains to be said that we can only do our best.

The Best Actions for the Worst Times

If I had my way, reality TV would feature mommy survivors— unsinkable Mommy Browns who are true grit in lip gloss, who steer logs through rushing rivers, and hand down to their bucka-roos noble examples of how to carry on in rough passages. To help you do your best in the worst of times, Elizabeth, Amanda, and Sally Jean and a cadre of my friends who moved beyond the un-thinkable offer their survivor recommendations below.

Talk About It

Whether you're feeling depressed or you hate your mate, whether your child has suffered a terrible accident or your husband has confessed an affair, the sooner you start talking, the sooner you'll free yourself of a stigma. Society is quick to blame wives and moms for whatever ails families, and blame is the last burden you need to carry around at a calamitous time.

"Talk to people about the difficulties happening in your life in a very matter-of-fact way," Elizabeth explains. "Don't be ashamed to tell people because, first of all, it isn't your fault. And secondly, people can support you once they know, and their support will be your lifeline."

Amid the strain of her husband's infidelity and failed marriage, Elizabeth didn't have the strength to throw Mackensie a first birthday party. But her friends insisted and carried out all the details, for which Elizabeth will always be grateful. "Women came out of the woodwork to offer help and support."

In addition to its consequences for a young family and a decade-long marriage, adultery devastates a woman's sense of self, her feeling of being attractive and sexual. For this situation especially, Elizabeth insists that being straightforward rather than hushed and private is a better strategy. Telling people allowed her to save face, and take control of the way in which she was being perceived by others at an incredibly vulnerable time.

Professional Talking

In troubled times, you may also need to talk to the professionals: a clergy person, a counselor, a support group, or your mother. Exposing denial, managing anger, and overcoming guilt and shame are critical skills for royally screwed-up situations.

Talking with a professional has other unforeseen benefits. As an example, Duke and I requested a tune-up with a counselor when I was pregnant with Liam. Three years old then, Patrick was famously rebellious, not abiding by the military-style commands my husband put forth. Which is why I felt justified at this session, launching into comprehensive complaints about my groom's behaviors, citing documents and providing detailed testimony.

As I talked, though, the counselor and Duke gradually recoiled in their chairs. The two of them tilted their heads and started look-ing at each other and at me as if I was a flesh-eating virus never be-fore identified on this continent. Evidently, my listing of complaints had turned into a vitriol attack—viciousness that ought to be re-served for Osama bin Laden and Ku Klux Klan members, not lov-ing, albeit clueless, husbands.

Although I can laugh about it now, this was one of the most jar-ring experiences I have ever had. I had stopped taking an antide-pressant when I got pregnant, but the counselor quickly concluded that depression was still a problem for me and a root of our marital rancor. She and her colleagues persuaded me that Prozac (the anti-depressant that has been most widely tested and proven safe in preg-nant women) was a wise choice for me and for my developing baby.

Although it's not widely known, depressed people often become unpleasantly aggressive, argumentative, and faultfinding without provocation. Mind you, Duke and our stressful life provided plenty of provocation, but I was also out of line without even realizing it.

Like nineteen million other Americans, you may be exhibiting boorish behaviors because you're depressed. Or you may be irrita-ble, distant, and thoughtless for one of many run-of-the-mill rea-sons. But a tone test, with a third party present whom you respect, is an excellent way to assess how far gone your diplomacy and com-passion might really be. In which case, the expert can help you get your marriage, your parenting, or your life off the skids with some healthier thought and behavior patterns.

In hard times, talk to your friends, both to elicit help and re-duce shame. Talk to a counselor or group to get your head on straight, your communication polished. And finally, talk to your kids in a similarly calm and unemotional manner. As members of your team, they need an honest acknowledgment of the difficulty your family is experiencing—a way to explain it to themselves. Children model coping mechanisms you teach them, as my boys did during my migraine headache, employing techniques they'd seen me use when they were sick.

Outlast the Pain

Notice how Amanda and Joe remained calm and didn't catastrophize the situation at its start? They took a day-by-day approach, which was likely the only way a mom could manage the anguish her son experienced while treating his seared back each day.

During any adversity, individuals and families have to learn to bear pain, and take it day by day until it lifts. Sitting out the angst and pandemonium, without resorting to talk of divorce and without telling your kids you wish they'd never been born, is incredibly difficult. How can you remain still when your heart is pacing the hallway and your high standards and dreamy illusions have removed the screens and are jumping out the second-story windows? We all believe we must *do* something to right a terribly wrong passage of living.

The Role of Faith and Time

This is where faith often intercedes and lends you strength. Not because you ask for it, but because you remain in the pain, not knowing what to do and simply being a vessel for whatever goodness or strength arises. Delay making big decisions and put off friends or relatives who push you for pronouncements. Don't overreact to tensions of the moment.

I have learned that when doubts, like shadows at sundown, grow big enough to engulf our bedroom, I must ask myself, do I want to be married? Do I want to do a little something to sustain this marriage so I have a mate with whom to share my life when the boys are taller than I am, pursuing adult lives and careers in the Peace Corps, NASA, or the World Wrestling Federation? My commitment to an oasis of companionship so seemingly far in our future, makes me work to retrieve our marriage from the dumps, time and time again, and put it right.

Last night, over bottled waters and chocolate, a friend told our mompool about her husband's increasingly dreary job prospects, her treasured nanny's recent departure, and the prospect that, to save money, she may have to serve as her husband's secretary—or office manager, we insisted calling it—for a while. The change ahead understandably overwhelmed her, although she lauded her husband for the initiatives he'd taken to find more work and for the loving care he provided for their two kids.

I had to intercede at that point and lovingly point out, "Is this the same husband you were berating a couple months ago for never doing anything? You know, for being, in effect, a non-contributor to the family in which you managed every single thing?" To her blushed face and guffaws, I said, "Wow, he's made great progress!"

She laughed and the room roared with recognition. Because all of us in early motherhood feel one moment that we're headed for divorce, a cliff, or a gated community where there are lots of psychiatrists, only to discover a few months later that the crisis has passed and we've wobbled ourselves upright again.

The Role of Failure

This is not the image I had of my life when I was a pious overachiever. I used to think that mealymouthed people who cited "unexpected setbacks" weren't pushing hard enough for change, or simply needed a rationalization for their failures. Only recently have I figured out that failure and pain is, in fact, the point.

Trying and failing. Mustering the strength to try again and failing. Trying again and succeeding, albeit in a different way than you expected to. Learning to hold fast and creatively tunnel through terrible accidents, volatile marriages, awful moods, thwarted ambitions, sibling tit-for-tats, and every other blip makes for a winning life. Sitting still in a quagmire, waiting for time to restore the sand to its place, or for nothing less than a miracle to occur, is not settling for less.

Like the chaos theory, in which physicists tell us there is some natural pattern even to seemingly arbitrary events, the precariousness of relationships that circle around youngsters will only amass sense in retrospect. So jolted are you during this period, you can't see that your marriage and family are developing shock absorption and resiliency worthy of a patent.

As a child watches you roll with the punches, she learns to be a survivor, too. She learns that values and tensions come tangled, and that yin and yang are like stripes on a barber's pole constantly recycling themselves in life. Like you, she learns to endure disappointments, injustices, and heartbreaks and to emerge wiser, kinder, and devoted to the lifelong task of counting her blessings.

In your trying moments, think of Amanda tending to her son's back day after day, setting aside ghastly flashbacks of the accident to focus on healing and the days to come. Feeling as if she was being gossiped about in the fishbowl of her community, she allowed herself to be embraced and supported by loving women. The wounds did finally close, and her son giggles and sleds again unaffected, those torturous daily dressings now a fading memory.

Kids Are Resilient

Sally Jean's story is far from that of a mother frustrated by not being the perfect PTA volunteer or the most patient math tutor. She had a son taken away from her for good; she was not admonished by a preschool teacher the way one mother I know was when her three-year-old kept "falling down too early on 'Ring around the Rosie' and pulling all the other kids down with him."

I'm not telling Sally Jean's story to diminish the frustration middle-class moms feel, but to put into perspective the way many of us overthink and overparent. The standards to which we hold ourselves contribute to the enormous tension we feel, and underestimate a child's fervent desire to be a team player and to help manage family life and its complications. Most moms I know don't think to delegate chores and they try not to bore kids on weekends with grocery shopping or errands. We're managing motherhood with white gloves when even in the roughest, dirtiest of circumstances, kids are astonishingly smart, sometimes even prescient. And in study after study, children prove amazingly resilient except in the most extreme of situations—poverty, abuse, frequent moves, several divorces.

I can't help but well up with tears when I think of third-grader Jonathan telling his mommy how proud he is of her, sensing as he does how important his forgiveness is. And Amanda told me that even with third-degree burns, with intravenous lines snaking away from his tiny arms and his torso wrapped like a mummy, Justin put on sunglasses that his cousin had made from pipe cleaners, and mugged for everyone in his hospital room.

In my case, as years of arguments and ultimatums cast over my husband's quick temper amassed, my sensitive and perceptive son Patrick suddenly began verbalizing everything he felt. "Daddy, I think you need to use your words more," he'd say. "Daddy, I love you but I don't like your behavior right now." There was no longer anything amorphous about the brain cells and ethical dough we were kneading. As regrettable as were our flaws, we taught Patrick a more important lesson: to share his feelings and trust that we would listen. In the end, we've learned, that is the best we can do.

Homeless and a teenage mother, Sally Jean dug through the trash to keep herself nourished enough to breast-feed her baby son. Many of us parent in a far more privileged world than that, and we need to trust ourselves and our kids to come through crises.

That's what families are for, after all: bearing each other's burdens and sheltering each other in squalls. You'll be surprised how significant a contribution a small child can make to a team, and to the abiding spirit that carries you through your worst days.

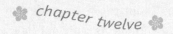
chapter twelve

The Perfect Mediocre Marriage

Riding Out Tumult and Embracing an Ordinary Life

SECRET: *A downgraded marriage is fine for family life.*

If marriages came with bond ratings, Wall Street would downgrade couples the minute they emerged from hospital lobbies with our burrito-wrapped babies in elbow-straining car-carriers. Because marriage with children is risky business, nine times more conflict-ridden than before kids come along and considerably handicapped in conversation and anything resembling a sex life.

As new moms, single women also experience a radically compromised quality of life. To accept and learn to love this new modus operandi, read on. When this chapter focuses on the nurture of relationships, know that your self-nurture is critical—for the sake of your little one and your sanity as his or her sole provider.

In marriages, Duke purports, the downturn starts nine months before birth, when the expectant mother foregoes alcohol. Husbands think it's a great deal at first, always having a designated driver. But it quickly becomes clear that abstinence from the traditional romantic precursor of wine or champagne is the first of many wet blankets heaped on your merriment.

Next comes a host of physical impediments. Sexual healing is highjacked by giant bellies, breast milk a-go-go, and hormones that say no, no for a long, long time. Robbed of sleep and energy, late-night movies and parties that start at nine are nixed, as are midday adventures—hikes, shopping sprees, football games, and the like— that might interfere with baby's, and thus Mom's and Dad's, nap. Travel beckons at first, until you spend your first night with a demon child screaming at you in a hotel room from her portable crib. From that point on, you realize "family vacation" is an oxymoron, and that staying home with side trips to the playground, monotonous as that is, is all your blood pressure can handle.

Money is tight so extravagant gifts and "trying out the new 'it' place" vanishes from the wooing scene. You've gained some pounds, so you don't have a wardrobe for "it" places anyway.

Personal calls from work are yanked, either because the spouse on the other end is interminably boring or because you're hyper-productive so as to leave at 5 P.M. sharp. Dinner talk is shouted into oblivion by your attention-hogging progeny, who also sandwich between you and your spouse whenever you try to hug.

Bedtime chats become logistics briefings or grudge matches, and goodnight kisses are impeded by the number of pillows you now have implanted under or between your knees or other aching body parts because you're aging parents raising relentless roust-abouts.

The Roots of Marital Mediocrity

For the first year, as comedian Paul Reiser jokes in *Babyhood,* spouses become more like sentries, and a brusque "It's your turn" signals the changing of the baby guard. Spending time alone together becomes a tad more feasible later on, except by then you may be so entranced with your offspring, or so used to your solitude that you refuse to let marriage reclaim its rightful role.

This is the mediocre marriage, not by trailer park standards of course, but several notches shy of the wow factor most of us associate with happy partnerships. We once aspired to Fred and Ginger fluidity and fun; now we stagger and slug the way a pair of tenth-round heavyweights do, leaning on each other to prevent collapse. And this extended stay in Dullsville causes many a couple to pause before their spiffy wedding pictures and ask, "Who are these smarmy people in princess dresses and tuxedos? And what on God's green earth are they so happy about?!"

This would all be so Hollywood Steve-Martin-and-Diane-Keaton funny except that divorce rates climb higher among couples who parent, with each additional child damning marriages proportionately. A national study conducted by the American Association of Retired Persons recently dispelled the myth that men in midlife crises, having found chicks who dig their new Harleys, dump their wives. Indeed, from age forty on, dissatisfied women are the primary instigators of divorce, initiating the proceedings in more than two-thirds of all legal break-ups.

Nebulous Questions in the Age of Un-Reason

Lackluster as love relationships become in the *Kiddotortureus* era, marital extinction can be prevented. Yet it's often difficult for us, as couples in the hot seat of parenthood, to gauge whether compromises are appropriate or whether we've sunk too low. Have you relinquished your high expectations for your marriage out of practicality or despair? Are you finally accepting your spouse for whom he is or giving up on being fulfilled by your relationship? Which accommodations are truly required to survive and which truly endanger your love?

In dating life, there was the proverbial unanswerable: Am I *settling* by going out with this guy or am I being practical, accepting that everyone has baggage? Nebulous questions like this bombard new parents, and the speed at which they come at us is quadrupled.

Marriages Erode

It's natural for marriages to evolve. Time teaches us to discern what we really want from what we wanted at first blush. We value less the glossier qualities that once throbbed with importance.

Scarier though, is when marriages erode. Tiny strands of connection slip away without notice. Chunks of soul are lopped off, disappointments cutting jags where a fuller love once stood. A hurting friend stood on a sidewalk outside our children's preschool and asked me, "How could my husband have gone back to work the day I lost my beloved grandfather?"

A mother in Boise, Idaho, agonizes over years of neglect that preceded her husband's request for a divorce. She reflected, "I see now how consumed I was with the kids and with being there for them. I should not have let motherhood take me over. I should have also worked at being an interested and interesting spouse." Lucky for her, she got a chance to redeem the lapses when her husband came home to try again.

Very deep disappointments encroach on marriages over time, as we discover no one can be a soul mate all of the time. Like camels, parental souls travel weeks at a time without refreshment and rarely have enough spirit to share. So the rush you felt being known for the first time turns into a lasting sting of being known for years but dismissed. Affection you never dreamed being uttered to you is supplanted by words exchanged in anger to which you never dreamed you'd stoop.

It's almost better to stay perpetually stressed and busy than to take time to consider the valuables you've tossed overboard to lighten the load on your drooping balloon of a marriage. When you do take a moment to assess the change, the list of losses is long—some bitter, and others causing concern because you don't even mind having lost them.

Have I Caved or Compromised?

I no longer clamor for Duke to read my writing, much less hang on his words of praise or criticism. I insist on combing the kids' hair but don't really notice that my husband leaves the house with bed head. Should I be worried that I no longer crave his opinion, or anticipate how people see him in relation to me? Which is worse—the fact that goodnight kisses are gone, or that I don't feel compelled to bring them back?

Harried mamas don't have the luxury to think through overtures, or linger with friends over perplexing romantic dilemmas the way we did when we were dating or newlyweds. Indeed, most new moms have only the vaguest sense of their marital health.

"There's never time to talk, or to just focus on the marriage," says a New Jersey mom with a four-year-old, a two-year-old, and one on the way. "I don't have much emotional energy left for my husband. He gets what's left over."

A Connecticut nonprofit administrator and the mother of two boys admits the odyssey of postpartum marriage is one of survival, without much time for postgame analysis. "Our relationship has been severely tested by parenthood, so that the foundation is stronger than I could have imagined before. As for the specific ways we've grown as a couple, I haven't a clue."

Most moms would welcome a formula or a checklist to keep the engine of their marriage going. Go out and start it up every couple days, no problem. Take it out for a decent two-hour freeway drive now and again, will do. Schedule a tune-up once a year, check.

Instead, you and your spouse work fourteen-hour days and then have to tackle a toddler's bedtime routine. When hubby wrangles with you over the methodology of getting Lily to take a bath or change into her pajamas, it's unlikely you'll have a constructive communication strategy at your disposal. You'll either bicker or sweep your complaint under the rug.

Keeping Parenthood Marriages Intact and Thriving

Under blighted conditions such as these, marriages do well to stem the bleeding, much less do no harm. But most of us aspire to a far higher standard—the exceptional marriage in which intellect and passion are at a peak for both partners, not the dumbed-down version whose only aspiration is day-to-day survival. And none of us have any time to work on a marriage, much less mold it into an art form of museum quality.

Lucky for us there are plenty of forms healthy, happy marriages can take, as Judith Wallerstein and Sandra Blakeslee showed in the groundbreaking book *The Good Marriage*. And many of these forms are accessible by mere mortals, and pooped moms and dads.

Like most couples who were contented with the way things used to be, you probably can't fathom that it's wise for a marriage to morph. But if you think of marriages the same way you do Tinkertoys, you see that there are an infinite numbers of ways to assemble creative—and often fantastic—architecture.

"For a good long while, your marriage is going to be thrown off balance," advised a Washington, D.C., mother of three. "Be patient and trust that things get back to normal. They will."

I wouldn't say "normal," nor would many of my girlfriends who are still searching their mommy brains for terms to describe their listless but devoted marriages. But the pendulum that swings so far the first two years of parenthood can be brought back closer to center. And although you're unlikely to break any track records for marriage performance in the parenthood league, a satisfying and family-affirming relationship suited to you and your mate is within a tired mom's and dad's ability to maintain.

Don't Be Ashamed

A glass of wine or two into a double date, Duke and I find that dinner companions often confess their state of minds from an hour before—the tension of getting out the front door, rushing SpaghettiOs from microwave to the dinner table, and separating from children left with babysitters. More often than not, we find our friends drive to restaurants and dinner parties the same way we do, aggravated at each other, sighing heavily, and finding tremendous interest in the car door handle so as not to make eye contact with their spouses. In a candlelit place among friends, when a wash of relaxation comes over us like a wave of hormones, our view of the entire planet is brighter, softer, and kinder.

Even without alcohol, you can summon a less fazed, softer-lens focus on this segment of married life. The incantation starts with realizing you have nothing to be ashamed of. Turmoil is incredibly common among couples who have, in recent years, welcomed willful sprites into their lives.

You Aren't Crazy After All

Carolyn and Philip Cowan, University of California Berkeley professors and the foremost authorities on the parenthood transition among married couples, say this is one of the most powerful benefits of groups they sponsor for expectant and new parents. "When our group members learn, in the presence of other couples just like them, how common these shifts are to this period of life, they stop taking them personally," Carolyn says. No longer feeling inadequate as individuals or as a couple, they are more likely to engage in "collaborative problem-solving than adversarial sniping."

Not only was squabbling reduced but expectations were also reduced, so that couples could set the bar more appropriately and work on enhancing the relationship with baby steps, which were also more apt to be successful. Talking about intimate subjects also proved important, because tired partners who weren't making notches in their bedposts could stop worrying that something was terribly wrong with them and turn their attention to the entertaining work of making better whoopee.

Minute-to-Minute Marriages

In many ways, this is the cause to which this book is dedicated: creating a genre of ridiculous motherhood and parenthood stories that make you feel at home in a life you might otherwise be embarrassed to call a life. With these stories of scattered lives and minute-by-minute marriages, we forge a medium even more compelling than the celebrity fairy tales woven by *InStyle* and its TV cohorts.

Here's an example from my topsy turvy marriage: I am sprawled on the floor of an aisle at Home Depot, holding back tears and becoming one with that dark place inside that can't believe a marriage could sink this low. Duke has flung an opened container of parts on a shelf near me and stormed off into the great unknown of hardware superstore aisles. That's because I dared ask, in front of sweaty contractors and saw-dusted amateurs, "Are you sure you know what you're doing? Shouldn't we just call a locksmith? We really can't live without a lock on the front door for another two weeks."

In a rush to get home to relieve the babysitter, we have tackled a task with the highest degree of difficulty: a household repair. Furthermore, Duke says angrily, I have "upbraided" him in front of his tool-toting brothers, a form of humiliation topping all others. In my worldview, I am the battered wife, left to pick up the inner workings of a deadbolt, and wonder what the hell the term *upbraided* means.

Merely three hours later, the lock is fixed and the boys are in bed—their cheeks flushed with warmth and peace. The house is a sweet haven again, our bed decadently comfortable, and Duke flirts with me. We laugh at the ridiculousness of the term *upbraid*, of the extra syllables Duke employs and the vocabulary words to which I was not exposed, despite my top-notch English degree.

My breath evens with the contentedness of it all. As it has so many times during these last several years of parenthood, the milieu changes by the millisecond.

Most of my friends in this stage of life are in wildly comical marriages, unable to rest on love laurels because the tensions brought about by our adorable hooligans are always exposing our weaknesses. We've been witnesses to each other's marital spats. And we've been each other's support network, hosting a sleepover or a play date so a time-starved marriage can takes its medicine.

Mostly we acknowledge that stress is the culprit, turning good people into temporary gremlins. As years go by at the playground, and our children go from baby swings to big-kid swings, we see many marriages endure dark periods and rebound in a hard-won happiness.

Sure, there are Stepford Wives in my neighborhood who play the suburban card game bunko and who act as if everything is always perfect. They may consider Duke's and my foibles, and those of others from the playground, kindling for great gossip. But I've stopped believing there's some pearl of a marriage just behind the curtains of the prettiest house on the block. And I'm staying busy, retying the knots around my own pearl, appreciating its own unique luster and flaws.

Rediscover and Rely on Your Leveler

A family therapist once explained to me, "New moms don't care very much about working at the marriage, except that they know they *should* care." When her children were very young, this same therapist remembers she felt utterly disengaged from her husband, except that she had a lot of trouble sleeping at night after they argued. "If I hadn't cared about the marriage, if I had truly been as disengaged as I thought I was, I would not have lost sleep over it."

Inside of most moms I know is something akin to a leveler, that thingamajig you use to hang pictures straight on walls. Keep the bubble in the fluorescent green fluid between the lines and you'll achieve a balanced effect.

In the off-kilter world of parenthood, I know it feels as if that leveling bubble travels to far-flung corners and revels in extremes. When he forgets your birthday, or worse yet delivers a card a day late, you squint at this man across your coffee cup and think, what's he good for anyway?

Invisible at First, the Leveler Weighs In

In the very early months and years of parenthood, it's enough to know the leveler is there, keeping your love within reasonable albeit broad boundaries. You shouldn't push yourself to right the scales of romance with silky negligees or love notes left in his briefcase. Later on though, you may need to quiet your preschooler's booming demands with, "Daddy and Mommy are talking now. You need to find something else to do for awhile."

When you tune in, the leveler can tell you that you're picking a fight because this is the tenth straight weekend you've spent exclusively with him and his progeny, and you are bored silly. So you know it's time to invite interesting people over, to plan a Saturday outing to a lavender field or a working farm, or to get your husband and your friend's husband together for a day of golf.

Unfortunately, the leveler also asks you to perform exorcisms, to return to your spouse and rescind that brilliantly conceived argument you made two days ago. Instead of feeling smug that you're the superior partner, you're moved to tell him, "When I said you *always* find ways out of helping me with bathtime, I neglected to mention how much more you've been pitching in lately and how much I appreciate it."

A love conscience exposes smoke and mirrors, too, and prompts you to confess at a calmer time, "That argument about sex the other night is really about much, much more than that for me."

Kids Won't Cede Attention

You should also know that children are the anti-levelers, as you've undoubtedly gathered every time you strike a perfectly good compromise only to have them whine "But that's not fair!!!!" Doe-eyed toddlers want you to dote on them to the exclusion of your spouse. A mommy at my tell-all sessions remembers she hated it as a child when her parents went out on Saturday nights. "But I'm so glad now, seeing my parents gah-gah over each other in their seventies."

Triangularization and Strangulation

Triangularization is the psychological term for the three-way attention match set off by the addition of a little one to a marriage. I often point out to couples in my expectant parents' classes at Babies "Я" Us that it's no coincidence the word looks and sounds so much like *strangulation*. Remember how jealous and nasty third grade became when you tried to fold your two best friends into a happy threesome? You're experiencing the same phenomenon in early parenthood, a tugging from two sides bound to strain and tear your Raggedy Ann arms.

But you really must correct the geometry and restore the ties that bind you to that third-point partner of yours. A friend shrank from the prospect of a date the next night with her husband. "I don't want to go out with him. What do I even have to say to him right now? He doesn't know who I am, he doesn't have the slightest idea how hard I'm working." She couldn't imagine that an evening out in which she and her spouse concentrated on fun rather than on the tedious logistics of everyday life, might alleviate some pressure and make it easier for them to communicate later on.

It reminded me of a time when I was single but in a heartbreaking relationship, walking on a Nantucket beach with a man who didn't love me. A woman my age was sitting glumly alone, looking on, and I wanted to run up to her and say, "This is a mirage. You think that I have it all. Except inside, I am devastated, and last night I lay next to this person in the moonlight and cried because none of the pieces are coming together."

Walking the beach with someone with whom you are bitterly out of sync is gut-wrenching. Except that over time, I've come to cherish the part of me that sides with hope, that reserves the beach-front room and the best table in the cozy Italian restaurant, and that forges the gestures of love and affection, even if for naught. This is my leveler, the believer in love that keeps trying, the believer that sex is important even if I have no desire, the believer that dates are critical even if Duke is driving me nuts.

The Balancing Act of Marriage

We may not always have the clarity of mind to know which compromises are good and which are devastating in long-term impact. John Gottman, the researcher who can predict with great certainty which marriages will thrive or fail, uses a ratio of simple kindnesses to small slights in his appraisal of relationships. He says good marriages internalize the mathematics and sense when the bad has outweighed the good for too long, when the civility has slipped, and when too much attention has shifted to the smaller members of the household.

Increasingly, moms look to talk show hosts, magazine articles, and even self-help books to cite and flag appropriate boundaries. But there's nothing in these pages that you don't already know, no topic that isn't already being hotly debated in the recesses of your heart and conscience.

Truth be told, I do still notice the times Duke goes out with bed head. And I note the absence of goodnight kisses, which I wouldn't if I didn't care. So it's time to let lip radar do its magic again, crossing the tower of pillows between us to plant kisses after the lights are out.

Maybe you, too, can unbutton your heart one button's worth and let tiny gestures of affection and concern tiptoe over to the man whose words and deeds sometimes seem superfluous. Next time you find yourself magnetically drawn to your child's head, worshipping each strand of hair as you do, take the triangle path instead to its farthest corner. Find the man: caress his receding hairline, his wrinkled brow, his hungry heart instead.

Cherish an Ordinary Life

Two lessons emerge when you spend several years resisting the duller adult life parenthood brings, and feeling the effects this recession has on your love life. The first is that ordinary life is probably a better teacher than dating was when it comes to sizing up great spouses and rehearsing a forever-and-ever romance.

That's why the new mom in the Berkshires who loved to go out to her husband's workshop and watch him work hasn't experienced a big decline in marital satisfaction. She's just pulled a rocking chair into the workshop for her and their baby daughter. There's solace for her, rocking and watching.

Boredom Is Good

Like the hand that can make a church and a steeple, or a grocery line shorter with several rounds of "rock paper scissors," the marriage that can stand still and find glints of interest in the stillness is buffered during this period and for the day-to-day life of several more decades. Boredom is good for marriages the same way experts tell us it's good for children.

When we are forced to be creative, we reignite the firing of nerve pathways in our brains, sources of imagination and free thinking long dormant because we're more accustomed to being externally titillated and excited. Instead of expecting fireworks to explode in the horizons of lives always topping themselves, you start looking around your own cabin for kindling, for twigs and brush that make sparks and colors dance in your own hearth.

Duke and I would rather dig into our pockets for coins to toss into fountains any day than keep filling the slots of video games. Making memories for our boys has become our favorite pastime, although I should point out that we're the lamest tooth fairies ever, falling asleep amid our reminder notes and botching our magic duty. We keep our sons patient, telling them the pixie in our zip code services a larger tooth constituency than most. But even these stories and the songs we make up to satirize "perfect parents" give our marriage an intimate language only we can decode.

Relearning Simple Fun

Our children have, of course, infused our household with open-mouthed "see food," with skating across the floors in sock feet, and with masterpieces fingerpainted in chocolate pudding. They've reintroduced us to simple fun. Years before the Red Sox overcame their legendary jinx and won the World Series, I was heartened at the faith of a six-year-old fan who declares to his classmates after a single victorious pennant race: "The curse is over! The curse is over!" How can you not be overcome with laughter while dropping "reindeer poop" raisins on the driveway to authenticate for two red-cheeked angels that Santa was really there?

No matter how stressed children make you, no matter how eager you are to see them in bed, minutes later you will have to tiptoe in and see their tranquil sleeping. You and your partner will be moved to hover above their exquisite heads, to watch twitches taking place in dreamland, and to breathe in the mist rising from deep, quiet pools of content.

I confess, I could have lived without trailing a garbage truck for five blocks in a hot, smelly alley, with Patrick waving nonstop at the trash guys and squealing each time the truck's mechanical arm clasped and dumped a can. But I would not have left God's green earth without seeing Duke, each night before bed, play "trash truck" with his two tiny sons. With fantastic sound effects and mimelike robotic movements, Daddy lifted them upside down, high over his head and triumphantly dropped them onto their beds and into fits of giggles. "Again, again, Daddy," we all clamor.

Just Like High School: Cheap Dates

Play is such a great skill for marriage. Having been sideline soccer and hockey moms, two women I know have taken up these sports themselves in adult leagues, playing on teams in their late thirties and early forties. Their husbands are now in the stands, cheering on these sexy, brazen brides.

Duke likes to show me "he's still got it," flirting with cute girls and waitresses. Of course, the irony is that he's working his little boys for every bit of *their* charm, walking them around restaurants and teasing comments out of enamored, albeit maternal, women.

My miserly girlfriends have invented hundreds of rock-bottom cheap date activities, a portion of which appear in the sidebar on page 222. Here, suffice it to say a coupon book can turn a date into a scavenger hunt of new places and great bargains.

Getting Away

After a weekend away from her two kids under age six, a friend of mine can't stop raving about the deliverance made possible by a Napa bed and breakfast. She sends an email out to all of us parents recommending the place, the zeal of a new believer in her pitch. If sleeping in, room service, and spa treatments felt decadent before, today they are curative. These regimens are so healing that your addled brain can't even articulate what "getting away" meant to you, only that you feel vastly, vastly better, reacquainted really with the people you once were and the love you once lavished on one another.

Yes, when we went to London and Scotland a couple years ago, Duke and I commented incessantly about how we wished the boys could see the Tower of London, hear its dark history, and stand next to its knights in armor. In the stalls of a Portobello flea market, we bought an extra suitcase to carry home all the booty we'd collected for them.

But Duke and I also remarked, as if possessed, on how *incredible* it was to be alone, to have ten full days to languish in each other's company and wander aimlessly through museums and sheep-grazed hills. After years of feeling stagnant and stupid, I fingered the engraved tombstones of my literary heroes John Milton, Henry James, and the Brontë sisters in Westminster Abbey, feeling the hairs on the back of my head rise with awe. Only Duke could know, having felt the same surge of pleasure tasting whiskey in a distillery in Oban, how much those extravagances fed my soul. On this higher plain, our marriage and our individual souls need to make memories, too.

Learning and Teaching Moderation

In *The Blessing of a Skinned Knee,* author Wendy Mogel explains that in a spiritual sense, it's healthy for kids to want things.

As greed-driven as it seems when children obsess over Power Rangers or Barbie airplanes, Mogel suggests children are only responding to the abundance of the universe, the largesse of life provided for us by a generous creator. We must teach children to become moderate consumers and responsible citizens of wealth but Mogel suggests we do so without shaming them for wanting things in the first place.

The hungers inside of couples are good, too. We should want to see Paris in springtime, to spend weekends together at more fantastic places than playgrounds. We should want our adult lives to be full and robust, and it's natural for us to feel deprived when a child we adore nevertheless takes from us freedoms and pleasures we also cherished.

The conservative movement tells us we are bad parents for being raised to fulfill ourselves, having been conditioned to seek not honor or sacrifice but our own destinies. But we need not feel browbeaten as a generation for wanting it all, and I no longer feel ashamed about being passionate, a voracious lover of learning and trying new things.

Yes, I get furious that I cannot put my arms around everything I love. So instead of banging out the notes of a mean concerto, I must let a finger fall on one single piano key at a time, letting each lovely tone reverberate in me. But what a bounty, to never be sated, to always want more of life's offerings, which motherhood, the demands of careers and small children only let me have in baby spoonfuls.

It's our responsibility to be good stewards and to manage well our palates for all life has to offer. In that vein, an ordinary life does teach you to weave straw into gold. But it also teaches you the precious nature of gold. With marriage, as in all things, moderation is a benevolent and wise teacher.

20 Cheap Dates
Courtesty of My Bargain Romance Experts

"Go to a batting cage, putting range, or play pool at a bar. Competition makes you feisty."

"Take a walk somewhere scenic and hold hands."

"Take in a matinee. Take advantge of early bird specials or happy hours at restaurants and bars."

"Have a picnic at a free outdoor concert, in a rose garden, or a sculpture garden."

"If you can stay awake long enough for it to get dark, take in a drive-in movie. Steam up the windows."

"Drink wine and do some stargazing on a blanket or sleeping bag in your backyard."

"Tickets to community theatre are very inexpensive and shows are quite entertaining."

"Plan a progressive dinner with friends and neighbors. Pool the kids and babysitters together at one house."

"Have dinner at home with the kids, then go out for dessert and coffee."

"Take a class together, such as wine appreciation or gourmet cooking."

continued . . .

"Go to open mike nights or amateur hours at local coffeehouses or bars."

"Have a spa night at home. First we do back massages. Then we dip each other's feet and hands in paraffin."

"Find a make-out point and watch the submarine races."

"Join a couples group at your church or synagogue. Oftentimes they offer child care for concerts and events."

"Get a sitter and do a house improvement or yard project together. It's nice working together and gratifying to get something done."

"Go holiday or birthday shopping for the kids. Then come home, drink eggnog, and wrap gifts together."

"Rent a paddleboat or a canoe at a local lake. You'll be amazed how quiet it can be at dusk."

"Spend an evening at Ethan Allen or Restoration Hardware trying out each chair and couch, planning your dream home."

"Relax in a café, reading books aloud to one another."

"Put the kids to bed and undress each other in a closet."

❀

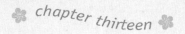

It Gets Easier . . . Sort Of

Graduating from Novice to Veteran Parenthood

> SECRET: *Admire and celebrate how far you've come. What a beautiful mom you are!*

Yesterday, when I took Patrick to school, I learned that his teacher for the next academic year had already been chosen without my returning the input form I was supposed to fill out. Then I dropped Liam at his last day of preschool and realized I'd not yet bought end-of-school-year teachers' gifts, much less presents for each of his classmates, as several moms had. By nine o'clock in the morning, I was already neck-deep in guilt and joking at my own expense that I'd never be "mother of the year."

It was a typical day, dividing myself between tasks, none of which get done to my standards. I apologized to my literary agent for being late delivering this chapter; I apologized to my husband for giving him unwrapped birthday presents; I apologized to a friend whose urgent call for play date help had gone unheeded; and I apologized to the kids for not reading books because I'd let them stay up too late watching TV. Without the sesame oil I'd forgotten to buy, I said to myself, the pork chops for dinner were sub-par. Oh, and I told my husband he'd have to take a rain check on that special birthday sex he looks forward to all year long.

Holding my hand in the dark, Duke nevertheless told me how much he adores me and what a great wife and mom I am. The hours of degrading self talk into which I had descended began to lift. I was glad I had dedicated the cake we had for dessert to both Duke's birthday and the citizenship award Patrick received at school. I was glad I read the tea leaves of Liam's deviant behavior and took time off from my writing crunch to spend with him—attention he lapped up and loved. I was grateful that the friend I couldn't help had called me earlier in the week thanking me profusely for another fa-vor I'd proffered. The balance sheet tallied, I let sleep and the love of my family wipe the slate clean again.

Please, Tell Me It Gets Easier!

All of us engaged lovingly and exhaustively in early parenthood want to know, *When does it get easier?* Does the feeling of doing everything half-assed diminish when your child turns three, or six, or sixteen? Is it easier when you have only one child, or will a sib-ling playmate simplify matters? Does the energy you had for your marriage return at some point? Do the pace of life and the number of details to handle become more manageable?

I know you are all holding your breath, waiting for me to ex-claim, "Yes! Only one more year of this torture and poof, life gets in-credibly sane again! You get your body back, only skinnier! You get ample sleep and sex! You become a wonder parent, never relying on TV as a babysitter. Your memory becomes a steel trap, your values an unwavering beacon by which your child navigates all of life!"

Painfully, I have to inform you that, according to a cadre of parents with grade school– and middle school–aged rugrats, the pace does not slacken. Nor is there a reprieve from a social life made up almost exclusively of children's Saturday afternoon birthday parties.

The Wonder Years of Three and Older

However, here are the gains you can expect. At the three-year mark, a child's immunity typically strengthens and there's a reduction in the mucus torrents, ear infections, and resulting sick days. And for those of you who fear that potty training will extend into college, diapers do eventually disappear.

A toddler or preschooler is increasingly able to tell you what she wants and needs, which makes parenting requirements more straightforward. It's also a big coup the first Saturday morning your previously needy morning owl is satisfied with a bowl of cereal and watching cartoons unaccompanied.

By year three, many moms and dads grow accustomed to functioning on less sleep. Moms regain some libido, short-term memory, and mental clarity while reaping added benefits in efficiency, confidence, and creativity. And as you see your little rascals grow, make friends, learn to read, pick right from wrong, make cereal necklaces, and paint flowerpots for you, parenting becomes a richer experience. Your child begins to convey to you and to others the lessons and love you've imparted, his character traits emerging with your imprint.

From Kindergarten On

At the kindergarten milestone, you can raise a glass to the reduced costs of child care, if indeed you've selected a public school. An older child can also go places and take part in activities that are remotely interesting to adults, graduating from the interminable Candy Land to competitive checkers, from eating and throwing sand at the beach to chasing waves and squirting you with a Super Soaker.

As highly touted as Baby's first words or steps, the "firsts" that come in later years are astonishingly meaningful and fun. It's incredible the first time Scotty serves as the accolade at church, the first time Brittany accepts a trophy from her tee ball coach, and the first time Gus reads a book to you. I'll personally never forget how enthralled Patrick was, telling me the story of Harriet Tubman and the underground railroad, or how he sang "Food, Glorious Food" for days after seeing his first live musical, *Oliver*.

Start Over with Another Baby?

'Bout the time you start to adjust, or earlier in the pressure-cooker time frame enjoyed by parents of "advanced age"—as obstetricians term those of us over thirty-five—the baby urge can get rather insistent.

There are definite advantages to having a second child. The sheer demand for extra arms can force fathers to step forward and share more of the house and parenting work. You'll be more confident with subsequent imps, too, which makes the whole baby stage much more enjoyable. And siblings sometimes do keep each other occupied, although they can also bicker and fight, scream and bite so much you become their full-time referee.

Duke and I decided to have a second child in the most tentative of ways. We knew that our leaky boat could easily give way, acknowledged that parenting baby Patrick had taken us within an inch of our lives, but believed we had enough dogpaddling in us to give our son the significant gift of a sibling. Surprisingly, at least up until his rebellious years, Liam brought healing to our household. I escaped a second stint of postpartum hardships and Liam greeted Duke as if he was only a bosom away from being God's gift to babyhood.

Wrestling over the Number of Kids

Several moms I know have set numbers of children they always dreamed of having—numbers that realism has made them relinquish or that they are chugging towards determinedly, without regard for financial or emotional cost. A good friend of mine is abiding by a superstition that she has to have multiple children to compensate for some disappointing her later on. When she complains about her husband's lack of can-do helpfulness, it sounds to me as if she's decided to have children with her nanny, the more faithful partner.

A mother of an eight-year-old offers her wisdom, "I'm a very good mother of one. I enjoy my daughter immensely and spend a lot of time with her. I simply ignore all the talk about 'Who will she have when her father and I are dead and buried?' Because I'm not so sure I'd be as good of a mother to two or more."

A thirty-nine-year-old in my mompool is wrestling with the decision, nine months into life with her very amenable first child. "I can't afford to wait much longer. Listening to those of you who have more than one, I'm apt to think I ought to quit while I'm ahead. Maybe my baby urge will just go quiet."

"Or maybe it won't," says another mom, this one the proud owner of not one but three easy babies. "Nobody else has the right answer for you. You have to weigh the decision you'll ultimately be happy with. Because I've been out with my three children and had people say to me, 'Think you have enough kids already?' Whatever you do, somebody will have an opinion about it."

My friends and I disagree with Dr. Laura about most topics these days even though we guiltily enjoy tuning her in. But as our wise selves *and* our kids' moms, we do think she's right that when Dad says "no dice," the matter of more children has to be dismissed. Many of us with less than fully contributing partners now appreciate how much a family is handicapped by this. We know now that even the most loving of mothers cannot make up for a reluctant or worse yet, an antagonistic partner.

The Challenges As Kids Grow

Whether or not you deposit more of your bloodline into this planet of ours, the years ahead will have their share of child-related challenges. The blessings brought by increasingly verbose kids are also a curse, since much of the time your preschool-aged scamp will be more ill-tempered and vociferous than *Seinfeld's* Soup Nazi. At age three, children also tend to give up naps, the only thing that keeps many mommies I know from committing hara-kiri. Although if you're like my husband, you'll consider the nap gap blasphemous and establish hours of "quiet time," at least for Mom and Dad, on long, tiring weekend days.

Depending on the school, homework demands begin in kindergarten or first grade, with twenty minutes of your evening allotted to reading, on top of the other worksheets your budding genius may need help with. If you figure on an hour for dinner prep and wolfing down food, forty-five minutes for homework and reading, and another forty-five for baths and bedtime routines, you've got a jam-packed weekday evening, even without soccer practice or a quick errand. You will no longer expend as much energy turning tantrums into teaching moments, but the permission slips, lunch accounts, away games, holiday parties, teacher conferences, field trips, sleepovers, open houses, parades, spelling tests, and recitals deplete the sand and stamina in the hourglass just the same.

Working v. Staying at Home

Although you feel less like a degenerate working full-time when you have a school-aged child rather than a baby, the painful question of paid work versus home never really wanes. My friend Georgia in St. Louis worked full-time through the initial years of baby Shaina's life, never believing the science that suggested those were sacrosanct, formative years. "My daughter slept more than half the day for those first three years," Georgia says.

Now that Shaina's a purse-carrying third grader, Georgia works part-time and is home when her daughter arrives from school so she can lend a hand with homework, facilitate play dates, take her to dance lessons, and help out with Girl Scouts. "In so many respects, I feel it's more important to be home with Shaina now," Georgia says. "And when she hits the teen years, I *have* to be home. Because she's only going to open up to me once in a blue moon and I need to be available when she does."

It's common for parents coming out of the preschool years to suggest that their next big assignment in raising their brood isn't until the teen years. Even if that suggestion isn't quite right, reaching this plateau is reason for contemplation and celebration. It's time to take off your pack, take in the view, and appraise your accomplishments, which is what my friends and I encourage you to do in our parting wisdoms.

Celebrate Your Mommy Milestones

Receiving a standing ovation when she was introduced before a comedy performance, Ellen DeGeneres wishes the rest of us could get this kind of greeting at work. Imagine, she says, going into your office and having your co-workers hail you with a standing ovation.

Celebration: This is what we wish for all you moms, each time you achieve a milestone in this love-a-thon called parenthood. Our kids get gold stars and prizes every time they turn around—for doing their chores, for brushing their teeth, or for staying "on task" at school. It's high time there was a party for the women who keep whole families, finances, logistics, and value systems on task.

It's a funny thing, how modern moms are rebuked for being selfish and self-centered. Yet, all around are moms "who forgot to put themselves on the list," as Wyonna Judd once said in an interview with Oprah Winfrey. A singer, boss, wife, mother, daughter, sister, and friend, Wyonna's desperation to lose weight also signaled her desperate need for self-nurture—to add her own needs to the list of those she was responsible for meeting.

What if, instead of feeling badly for finding the adjustment to motherhood so difficult, you commemorated your growth? What if you kept a record, not just of your child's rites of passage, but of your own? When you consider the dramatic bell curve of lessons faced in early parenthood, you deserve your own "A"-studded report card with your name on it.

Ironically, when your child reaches grade school and starts gaining more independence, the feeling of having her pull away can also be quite wrenching. Just when you conquer your adjustment disorder and start enjoying the immensity of your child's need and affection, the kid moves on. So you need to celebrate now—if only to dull the ache of having to let go, little by little, of the precious child who's outgrown the tiny clothes in the toddler section.

Often you need other moms to rejoice mommy milestones. Our mompool congratulates a woman who cleans out the garage she's been trying to attend to for three years. We toast a mom for demanding that "someone else cook the holiday dinner this year." We've checked in on and lauded a mom for preserving her sanity, three months after her horrid in-laws moved to town.

Your Private Party

Honor your accomplishments on your own, too. In the time it takes for your son to locate his cleats and shin guards, or to drive your offspring back and forth to piano lessons, regard the girl in the mirror: the daughter, wife, and mom you've become. You've come a long way, baby.

In the beginning, if you're like me, you used the term *mom* deprecatingly among friends, making fun of the attention and care an apron-wearing sponge-brain was supposed to smother on little people. A few blink-long years later, "mom" has become adult shorthand for "I don't brake for indecision," "I shoot perfectionists on sight," or "I need pampering like you wouldn't believe."

I've grown to like my minivan and to prefer an evening spent puttering in the yard and watching the boys play in their tree house. I've gotten comfortable with not owning my identity, but with letting it be formed by tiny choices I make every day: by hydrangea I plant in the backyard, by the cashmere I find stroking the cheeks of my young boys, and by words I pick to make women feel more comfortable in their skin.

Feel the expansiveness of your own maternal heart. Isn't it amazing how much a heart can grow? Admire your stamina, as if from a few feet away. Step outside some summer night at bath time and eavesdrop on the giggles and splashes, the battles for bath toys and bubbles, and the everyday delight your kids experience in your home. That's a sound to keep repeating, to make your mantra, as you slip quietly into a deeper breathing, more peaceful mode of mothering.

Celebrating Your Half-Baked Marriage

This is the time to do a spot check of your marriage and celebrate what there is to celebrate. By kindergarten, marriages that have survived the Ironman triathlon of "lack of sleep, lack of sex, and lack of money" possess a Rottweiler breed of tenacity, a comfort in soiled surroundings, and the ability to communicate in rushed hieroglyphics.

It may be that with five to fifteen years of married life under your belt, you realize your investment is sound. Perhaps the volatility of parenthood has taught you to banish "never" and "always" from your spousal critiques; if you're especially evolved you may have stopped offering critiques altogether, unless solicited.

This may, however, be the time you face the fact that your husband's drinking problem is not going away, but getting worse. Or see that the job you believed would only temporarily cheat you of time with your college sweetheart and your twin girls, shows no sign of easing up. Or, perhaps you recognize for the first time the malaise that falls over the house once your daughter goes to bed. You get busy picking up the house, and he retreats to the Internet without a word. Now is the time to break the silence.

When kids are older, you can more easily fan the flames of marriage. You feel safer instituting more date nights and couples' weekends away. Indeed the first time the parents of your son's friend pick him up for a sleepover, you may not to know what to do with yourselves, or have trouble believing that someone would *volunteer* to take your child off your hands.

If you're like me, perhaps the biggest milestone of all is to accept that *this is your life,* rather than pine for the Hollywood version you dwelled on during your first thirty years. It's a milestone when you choose real life over the romantic ideals with which women are bombarded all our lives.

At his recent birthday bash, my mom and I watched Liam dig his finger into the side of a pristine cake long before it was time to cut it. Mom told me that as a young minister's wife, enlisted to slice cake at a wedding, a guest caught her licking the knife between servings. How we laughed, thinking about her white-gloved faux paus. And I've learned my children and I are part of something much bigger than ourselves: a proud tradition of icing lickers.

You're Only Hazed Once

The icing on *this* story, friends tell me, is that you are only hazed by motherhood once. When we first become mothers, we engage in a serious pity party about the downgraded nature of our adult experience. We're hit with major disillusionment about what we'll accomplish in our careers. We grapple with, writhe over, and make sacrifices we never dreamed we'd make—and that our spouses often don't consider making. As much as we love our babies, the experience is much more jolting than anyone leads us to expect, and mixed feelings make us worry there's something wrong with us.

I hate that we go through this, and that this entry into the stratosphere of motherhood shakes us so. But I believe that it is, for many of us, an inevitable journey. As M. Scott Peck says, "The truth is that our finest moments are most likely to occur when we are feeling deeply uncomfortable, unhappy, or unfulfilled. For it is only in such moments, propelled by our discomfort, that we are likely to step out of our ruts and start searching for different ways or truer answers."

The gargantuan emotional transition that sets in when you first become a mom and lasts a solid three to six years afterward is then *done, over with, hasta la vista, ciao.* You no longer give a moment's thought to bringing a store-bought cake to a party, going to work with plain, unpolished nails, or telling your son he's driving you crazy. You do what you have to do to survive, making far fewer apologies than you did at the start. You count your blessings; you hold your son or daughter close; and you move quickly beyond any terrible, horrible, no-good, very bad days that crop up.

In my book, and in the psyche of my girlfriends, this is a *giant* step forward. Because even as children run between my legs and make me feel as malleable as *The Iron Giant,* my inner equilibrium is stable, my footing now as big and secure as a Rescue Ranger's. Although we moms will always feel competing impulses, wanting to flee our mundane lives but staying for the unrivaled intimacy of family life, we are human again. After all, these dual impulses gnaw at every mortal—although I believe only mothers experience the extremes we do, feeling such devastating vulnerability and unsurpassable, protective love.

You're a great mom. A strong, smart woman. A fabulous wife and lover. And undoubtedly a patron saint to your friends as they are hazed by early parenthood. You will want more, I know. But truly, what more is there to want in life than to possess these qualities—these the mother-of-all great attributes?

Coincidentally, there's another panda pregnancy to celebrate. I heard this morning on the radio that our famous panda Hua Mei has gotten herself knocked up. The four-year-old born at the San Diego Zoo is now in China where zoologists showed her sex education videos to prepare her for "blind dates." Next, I hope they show her the same grainy home economics films we saw in junior high, in which mothers bake cakes in dresses and pearls and wave at kids on the backyard swing set, while smiling unceasingly albeit blankly ahead.

As intimidated as I once was by Hua Mei's perfect mom, I have gotten the hang of this motherhood thing. A den of sassy moms have taken me in and let me kvetch with them. Yes, the lug with whom I share a pen is strong on the outside but he's got a soft underbelly.

And my cubs? Like those at the zoo, they are so precious I think people should pay admission to see them. Instead, come the fall, if the teacher doesn't bar the door, my baby Liam will be high-tailing it to grade school for kindergarten, where third-grader Patrick will have to learn to share his campus. Their school mascot? The pandas.

Conclusion

Fashioning Your Own "Happily Ever After"

❀ Predictably, you overachieving mommies have stuck around for some extra credit reading. And my girlfriends and I are prepared to reward you, albeit not with the dreaded cheap party favor toys we all love to hate.

Here are a few wrap-up wisdoms we've gleaned from our term of office in the Land of Toys Underfoot.

Change Your Mind

Before I was a parent, I didn't understand the adage, "Never say never." But flexibility and the prerogative to change your mind, even dramatically, become a mantra for moms and dads trying to manage child-driven mayhem.

Martha Beck—a mother, author, and regular *Oprah* magazine

contributor—is a big proponent of changing your mind. She says that humiliation and shame—which are wildly prevalent in modern motherhood—are often indicators that our actions are not working in tandem with our beliefs. While she was pregnant, Beck learned that the baby growing inside her had Down syndrome. As desperately as she feared the societal humiliation of having an "imperfect child," Beck could not bring herself to give her son up.

So, unable to bring her actions in line with her assumptions, she had to modify her beliefs to match her behavior. In her *Oprah* column, she writes, "I began questioning the assumption that people with Down syndrome are imperfect. Like anyone else, they are perfectly themselves, as nature made them. Maybe the real defect lay in the belief that such loving and lovable people were defective."

Beck's humiliation evaporated, as she tried on new ways of thinking and discovered better fitting, albeit buried, convictions. This is, I think, what transforms modern mommies into happy, rather than shamed, imperfect excuses for mommies.

Modern society surely uses moms as its punching bags, but we also devote considerable time to knocking ourselves silly, internalizing doubts, fears, and injustices. Even when imposed standards feel wrong, wrong, wrong, we rarely challenge the assumptions. We just keep criticizing ourselves for not meeting defective standards. In motherhood, we believe each move we make forges our children's futures, yet we forget to pilot ideas, make short-term assessments and adjustments, and base long-term strategies on smaller alignments and successes.

So, my evolving mommy friends, experiment with a different tact. Reshuffle the variables until the math feels right to you, plucking x from its logical seating next to y, and formulating an equation that sets your family square again.

Know that in marriages and in children, whatever you resist will persist. Your day-to-day values may get shot through with holes out of respect for your larger good—the harmony of your marriage and the happiness of your much-loved youngster. It's quite like aerating your lawn: pulling up plugs of your soul, freeing up obscured nutrients so that your green, lush future is assured.

Paradoxes in Parenthood

For the long-term redemption of bossy and maddening three- and four-year-olds, it means finding ways to say yes, though your every inclination is to say no. With husbands you want to be around forever—even though their contribution to fatherhood consists of TV time and a college drinking anthem sung at bedtime—you must accept their limitations and pilot combinations of self-sacrifice and self-care to see your marriage through the intense child-rearing years.

In my short mama tenure, I've been twisted like a pretzel by paradoxes. Going back to work when my kids were little—not staying at home—bolstered my husband and thus, our family. Letting go of a treasured identity and exposing striations of pain, a more complex and spectacular geode of personality was fashioned. Loving my husband—and his considerable flaws—did what we're told we can't expect love to do: it changed him dramatically and made him a good and loving father.

The topper to all this is that last spring, I insisted upon renting a studio a few blocks away from home, and set up a Virginia Woolf–inspired "room of my own," which felt nearly as important to me as my plans to start writing again. Duke was none too excited about paying the extra rent, no doubt in part because he wanted *his own* private testosterone pit. But because I was vehement that I needed this writer's haven, he relented.

This studio was me, me, me: white, hammered ceiling tiles hung on the walls and a daybed was dressed in vintage popcorn chenille coverlets. All girl, all the time, it was my cherished spot for solitary thinking.

Strangely though, as the book progressed, I found myself writing more at home. I was drawn to the stories Patrick would tell fresh off the school bus. I coveted Liam's cheers of "Mommy! Mommy!" as our nanny brought him home from preschool and he caught sight of my car out front.

In the end, my true blue belief in independence gave way to my truer love—that of being connected. Instead of standing my ground and proving to Duke that I was right, I smiled at him in a knowing, woman's prerogative way and said, "I want to come home to write."

Moving out of that treasured studio and closing the door on the woman who liked to remove herself, I am now an integrated writer and mom, whose spaces are as messy, blended and contradictory as can be. In fact, my desk is populated with Play-Doh masterpieces Liam has left to "help me write."

Ultimately, this is what I wish could be true for every mom: an integrated self that thrives on paradoxes and stays attuned to deep, eccentric wisdoms, the way a child hears the reverberations of the ocean in a single seashell. When you follow your unconscious stirrings, as a child would, life unveils a marbled pleasure that tired mommies need more than just about anybody.

Take Baby Steps

The concepts we've covered together in this book are mammoth, the challenges they represent overwhelming in the course of lives already choked with unattainable expectations. But life is made up of infinitesimally small interactions and decisions that in the final analysis, you allow to either damn or deify you.

The sweeping bliss we imagine babies will bring proves instead to be a mixed lot of unprecedented highs and lows. The marriage we expect to become more endearing in the context of our own families often disappoints—even devastates—us with its rigid confines. The women and mothers we dream we'll be, get pounded by children's insatiable needs, till we can no longer count the sacrifices or appraise the gains and losses. We simply have to let it be.

All that most of us know to do in this situation is hunker down, stroke the backs of our dear children, infuse our relationships with occasional kind words and gestures, and sometimes treat our souls to a good movie or an aromatic bath. As much as we want to drive away, most of us choose to stay, and to prop our eyes open for the marvels we were promised.

This, it turns out, is exactly the right path. Because the act of staying put in the present reality—not wishing it away, or belittling what you have—can be transforming. When you are obliterated by the present and only able to muster faith in the future—an act that feels feeble at best—grace can work its way with you and help you find a greater comfort within.

In essence, this is mindfulness, perhaps the most challenging and most rewarding aspect of parenthood. Many times during early parenthood, you have to decide that the here and now, this plastic baby pool sampling of life, is where you want to be. *This is the marriage* you want to remain after your children are grown. *This is the lesson* you want your children to teach their children. *This is the metamorphosis* that promises to make you a happy, fulfilled, older woman.

Reap these great rewards by being steadfast, and doing your best to imbue everyday experiences with meaning or learning. By staying awake when you desperately need sleep. By walking block after block after a smelly garbage truck with your engrossed three-year-old son. By enduring mediocre sex and conversation with the man who used to thrill you. By accepting a lack of forward progress, and a dearth of big finishes and purely gleeful days.

A Marriage Redeemed

For several years now, I've tried to find the "ambivalence section" of Hallmark cards for the spouse about whom I forced enthusiasm on Valentine's Day. Then this year, after so many bitter disappointments and agonizing arguments, my noble husband made a 180-degree shift in favor of our family. He gave us a happy ending.

Around again came the holiday of love, which coincides by a week with our anniversary, but this time I could not find a card sentimental enough. I could not find poetry effusive enough or soft-lens photography pretty enough to say what I felt. In the end, I picked the dorkiest card I could find: one of rabbits in bathrobes serving each other breakfast at a tea table on a flower-filled veranda.

Imagine my surprise when my hard-won soul mate's card also featured bunnies, these two in Romeo and Juliet costumes—star-crossed lovers with long, floppy ears, Shakespeare staged in paw prints. I had the two cards framed—these two ridiculous rabbit tributes to cornball love and storybook illustrations our children have taught us are magical.

Enjoy Imperfect Moments

Frame these less than sophisticated moments. The hilarity of seeing your kindergartener hold up her skirt and expose her panties while performing "I'm proud to be an American." The dispute your son has with you when you say "I love you all the way to the moon and back" and he says, "I love you all the way to the moon and back three times over." The adorable lisp of a toddler with a grumbling tummy, saying, "Mommy, I hun-gee."

See the pristine icing on a birthday cake poked with finger holes and know these tiny hands, and their matching feet, should be the measures you steer your life by—at least for now. Keep sending your kite up in the wind, watching it crash and get tangled in trees till you find a current on which to sail. Pocket the wisdom acquired from your failures. Sit next to a mommy friend in church and roll your eyes in agreed dissent when the preacher tells parishioners to "choose happiness, it's as simple as that."

You know how hard happiness is, how much work it can entail for women. With this in mind, forgive yourself more often than you worry. Laugh more than you belabor decisions.

Be mindful of the little things you say, and the smallest gestures of kindness you share as they contribute to bliss incarnate, served to mortals on modest cake plates. When your sweet son or daughter succumbs and slumbers, dreaming big dreams in your overburdened lap, know that heaven is tiny and time-consuming and lies within your very grasp.

How to Start Your Own Mompool

✿ Modern motherhood is a big mess. If government won't cut us more breaks, employers won't offer more flexibility, husbands won't pitch in more, child development experts keep ratcheting up their expectations, celebrities maintain that motherhood is bliss 24/7, and playgroups become competitive rather than supportive, what are everyday moms to do to stay sane? Start a mompool, I say. Here, I share some insights into how a mompool can keep you dog-paddling through parenthood.

Q. **What is a mompool?**

A. Like a carpool, it's a group of moms who band together to make life for everyone in the group easier. A mompool can provide crisis help—chicken soup or babysitting when one mom gets sick, or proven strategies and support when a mom goes through a rough period. Unlike a playgroup, the emphasis here is on moms alone, and on caring for the women who take care of everyone else.

Q. Why do I need a mompool?

A. A mompool is a way of creating part of the community our moms enjoyed and that we sorely need. Moms today think we should do this very hard work alone. But if you have women who know intimately what you're going through and with whom you can share your true feelings without fear of judgment, you'll be surprised how much energy and support it affords you for work and family life.

Q. What does a mompool do?

A. My mompool is a group of ten moms that meets twice monthly on a weekday evening to share dilemmas and triumphs, problem-solve and cheer each other on. We start at 7:30 P.M., spend about fifteen minutes getting snacks and catching up. Then we go around the room and each mom rates from 1 to 10 how she is doing or how eager she is to share something with the group. The two or three moms with the highest priority numbers become the moms we focus on that night. We have a moderator who keeps the group on track and a secretary who arranges meeting places and phone chains if a mom gets into a tight spot and needs emergency casseroles, babysitting, hand-holding, etc.

Q. What other structures do you put into place?

A. We have some important ground rules: Everything we discuss is confidential and stays in the room. We promise to honor each others' experiences without judgment, every woman gets a chance to talk in the course of an evening, and we try not to interrupt each other. We also want the evenings to be as low-stress as possible so we urge hostesses to serve only store-bought snacks.

Q. **What do you talk about?**

A. Everything! Sometimes a mom is at a breaking point because her three-year-old is very aggressive, or because she isn't communicating with her husband. Sometimes moms are embarking on new ventures such as home businesses or volunteer fund-raising and they're unsure of themselves. Some moms want to celebrate losing three pounds or seek absolution for saying the "f" word in front of their kids.

Q. **What if I want to have a different kind of mompool?**

A. Go for it. Mompools can be anything you want them to be, as long as their mission is taking care of mom—not the kids, the house, your husband, etc. Stay-at-home moms may need a social outlet more than anything—women to have a glass of wine with to break through the isolation. Sometimes moms just need ideas—practical solutions that have worked for other moms and their families.

Q. **How do you form a mompool?**

A. Start with a core group of moms who you'd like to see more of. Then sift through others you meet, slowly asking women you like to join you. I'm in a group of Jewish and Christian women, some stay-at-home moms, some working; diversity works really well for us. But I tend to think single moms need a mompool of single moms and that for example, stepmoms, lesbian moms, and African-American moms have so many unique struggles that they would probably benefit from a specialized mompool.

Q. How do make sure that the moms you invite will be good for the group?

A. Moms who pretend everything about motherhood and family life is perfect tend to opt out of the pool themselves. They're better off in playgroups if it feels selfish to them to focus on themselves rather than on their children. One mom I know asked women what they liked to read and what they liked to do in their free time, to get a sense of the mother first.

Q. How do we get moms to be honest and not feel self-conscious about sharing their feelings?

A. Use this book as a resource! Have your group read a chapter or a section per week; the candidness in the book sets the tone. On my website, www.margstark.com, is a group discussion guide designed to get moms opened up and reaching out.

Q. Why do I need another obligation in my life?

A. You will be nourished so much by a mompool that it will not feel like an obligation. We have some sleep-deprived moms of young babies who nevertheless wouldn't dream of missing mompool. It becomes like oxygen; you have to have time with your mompool to keep going.

Q. Where did the name "mompool" come from?

A. A few years ago at a spa called Ten-Thousand Waves at the base of a mountain in Santa Fe, New Mexico, I got up my nerve to go naked into an outdoor hot springs a clerk told me was "bathing suit optional." There were separate facilities for men and women, and the lighting was low except for a full moon and a piñon-burning fireplace near the tub. When I looked around at these women in the moonlight, I was struck by how beautiful all of us were—whether or not we had big bellies or muscles, sagging or taut breasts. In the moonlight, our skin tingling in a cool wind and hot bubbling water, we were guileless and imperfect and yet so astoundingly beautiful. That's what a mompool is: a group of raw-soul moms, reminding ourselves what a glorious role we have in life and gaining energy from this pool to take out into the world.

Recommended Reading

❀ I recommend you read only a few child-care and development books in early parenthood because their contradictions and out-of-reach expectations often do more harm than good. But here are some books and resources you can trust—first, to reassure you that you're normal and second, to inspire you to great momhood. Snuggle with your little one at bedtime then, if you can keep your eyes open, savor these writings.

For great humor and thinking about modern motherhood

Brain, Child: The Magazine for Thinking Mothers. You can subscribe at www.brainchildmag.com.

Operating Instructions: A Journal of My Son's First Year, Anne Lamott (New York: Ballantine Books, 1994). While you're at it, read any and everything Anne Lamott has written including archived essays on Salon.com.

Expecting Adam: A True Story of Birth, Rebirth, and Everyday Magic, Martha Beck (New York: Berkley, 2000). Don't miss Martha Beck's other books and her monthly genius in *Oprah* magazine.

The Mommy Myth: The Idealization of Motherhood and How It Has Undermined Women, Susan Douglas and Meredith Michaels (New York: Simon & Schuster/Free Press, 2004).

If you are expecting a child

The Pregnant Woman's Companion, Christine D'Amico and Margaret A. Taylor (Attitude Press, 2002).

Women's Moods: What Every Woman Must Know About Hormones, the Brain, and Emotional Health, Deborah Sichel and Jeanne Watson Driscoll (New York: Perennial Currents, 2000).

The Girlfriends' Guide to Surviving the First Year of Motherhood: Wise and Witty Advice on Everything from Coping With Postpartum Mood Swings to Salvaging Your Sex Life to Fitting into That Favorite Pair of Jeans, Vicki Iovine (New York: Perigee Books, 1997). With her bits on diet and exercise, keep in mind she lives in La-La Land Los Angeles and her husband is an executive in the entertainment industry.

To get a grip on marriage

The Seven Principles for Making Marriage Work, John M. Gottman and Nan Silver (New York: Three Rivers Press, 2000).

When Partners Become Parents: The Big Life Change for Couples, Carolyn Pape Cowan and Philip A. Cowan (Mahwah, NJ: Lea, 1999).

What No One Tells the Bride: Surviving the Wedding, Sex After the Honeymoon, Second Thoughts, Wedding Cake Freezer Burn, Becoming Your Mother, Screaming About Money, Screaming About In-Laws, Maintaining Your Identity, and Being Blissfully Happy Despite It All, Marg Stark (New York: Hyperion, 1998).

Secrets of A Very Good Marriage: Lessons from the Sea, Sherry Suib Cohen (New York: Clarkson Potter, 1993).

Halving It All: How Equally Shared Parenting Works, Francine M. Deutsch (Cambridge, MA: Harvard University Press, 2000).

The Single Girl's Guide to Marrying A Man, His Kids, and His Ex-Wife: Becoming a Stepmother with Humor and Grace, Sally Bjornsen (New York: New American Library, 2005).

To be a sane mother with sane children

How to Say No Without Feeling Guilty: And Yes to More Time, and What Matters Most to You, Patti Breitman and Connie Hatch (New York: Broadway Books, 2000).

The Blessing of a Skinned Knee: Using Jewish Teachings to Raise Self-Reliant Children, Wendy Mogel (New York: Penguin Books, 2001).

Acknowledgments

❀ Mothering—and muttering a book into being—is best done with a hefty support network, which I am blessed to have. Lucy launched this book, taking me in each month for my writer's weekends. Syl wiped my brow during two gargantuan pushes: one that brought Liam into the world, and one that made me expose more and more of my vulnerable mommy stories. And an extensive contingent of friends, friends of friends, and absolute strangers shared harrowing tales of modern parenthood with me.

As I made my way to becoming a settled and happy mom, I tugged on ears and soaked shoulders including navy wife friends Angie and Toni; Mt. Holyoke/Boston wise gals Beth, Betsy, Amy, and Lisa; Kansas City homeys Diane, Madeleine, Alex, and Sloane; San Diego sisters Elizabeth, Kim, Lynne, Sharon; the Scripps contingent and the KCC women's group.

Sybil Stockdale, Marissa Robbins, and Sandy Solem, thanks for inspiring me to great momhood with your strength and can-do practicality. Also, bless you Katie Couric, for challenging Penelope Leach when she suggested all new moms hate going back to work; that short interview was nevertheless manna for me in the post-partum wilderness.

Saint Georgina, the Magers family, the Benchley Weinberger and Kensington Preschool staffs, I have been so privileged to have you as partners, caring for and shaping my boys with your love, values, and stamina. Susie Walton, thanks for restoring Valentine's bliss by helping Duke and I find a parenting style we agreed upon.

Having Michelle Howry as an editor is as much fun as looking for vintage finds at an antique fair, which she knows is tops on my fun list. She and the great team at Perigee took great care in polishing this pearl and gave it great luster.

Brava to my agent and friend Laurie Abkemeier. Your anecdotes, lioness protectiveness, great ideas, and generosity of spirit made both the book and the making of it a pleasure. Here's *my* secret: You're my favorite agent, too! (Okay, so you're my only agent, but let's not quibble . . .)

To my mompool, you awesome women you, thanks for stuffing the entrails of my mommy brain back into my skull and making me laugh so hard that I need to do more kegels. Audrey and Risa, you have seen my family at its most Jerry Springerlike extremes and nevertheless keep bringing us meals and letting your kids play with mine. I'm deeply grateful.

My sister, Catherine, you were the wise-cracking, near-tears foundation on which this book was built. (May your good 'ol boys, Taylor and Spencer, not remain obsessed with monster trucks for long.) To repay all your love, Mom and Dad, I've delivered two rootin' tootin' grandboys. Otherwise I'd be doing dishes into perpetuity.

. . . Which brings me to my hunka hunka burning love, Duke.

You are my sweetheart, my partner in poor tooth-fairying, my generous and un-self-conscious mate. Thanks for letting me share our story to help others, even though I did have to pay you off with a home theater system.

Finally, for my little princes, the boys who drive their Sunday school teachers to drink, I have only one prayer. Know that whatever gigantic holes there are in your dad's and my character, and whatever toothpaste globs, chewed-up contact lenses, aced spelling tests, or letters from the principal you produce, you are my sunshine, my only sunshine.

index

About the Author

A magazine writer and author, Marg Stark is the mother of two outrageously energetic boys under the age of ten. Accordingly, she also serves as homework consultant, LEGO engineer, birthday party planner, and school fund-raising volunteer. She's written two previous books, *What No One Tells the Bride: Sex After the Honeymoon, Second Thoughts, Wedding Cake Freezer Burn, Becoming Your Mother, Screaming About Money, Screaming About In-Laws, Maintaining Your Identity, and Being Blissfully Happy Despite It All* and *Timeless Healing: The Power and Biology of Belief* with Herbert Benson, M.D. Stark's first magazine article—about two men living and dying with AIDS—was adapted into a NBC television movie, *Roommates*.

Stark graduated from Mount Holyoke College, got her masters in journalism from Northwestern University, and a lot of life lessons as the daughter of a liberal Presbyterian minister and the wife of a conservative U.S. naval officer. In 2003, *Metropolitan* magazine selected her as one of San Diego's "40 under 40" most accomplished leaders. A first-time mom at thirty-three, Stark fell in love with her strawberry-blonde babes but was wildly disoriented and humbled by the adjustments to motherhood. She, her husband, Duke, and their boogie-boarding fanatics, Patrick and Liam, live in a fixer-upper Craftsman in sunny San Diego, California.